Warrants

Analysis and Investment Strategy

Donald T. Mesler

Probus Publishing Company
Chicago, Illinois 60606

This publication is designed to provide accurate and authoritative information in
regard to the subject matter covered. It is sold with the understanding that the
publisher is not engaged in rendering legal, accounting or other professional
service. If legal advice or other expert assistance is required, the services of a
competent professional person should be sought.

FROM A DECLARATION OF PRINCIPLES JOINTLY ADOPTED BY A
COMMITTEE OF THE AMERICAN BAR ASSOCIATION AND A
COMMITTEE OF PUBLISHERS.

Library of Congress Cataloging in Publication Data

Mesler, Donald T.
  Warrants : analysis and investment strategy.

  Bibliography: p. 185.
  Includes index.
  1. Stock warrants. I. Title.
HG4028.S82M47   1985   332.63'22   85-25789
ISBN 0-917253-25-6

Library of Congress Catalog Card No. 85-25789

Printed in the United States of America

1   2   3   4   5   6   7   8   9   0

2294442

To my mother and father.

PREFACE

More warrants are trading now than at any point in history. The current environment—a strong stock market, frequent merger activity, an interest in new issues, low (by comparison) interest rates, and a pressing need for companies to clean up their balance sheets—are all conducive to the issuance of warrants.

The proliferation of warrants has taken place without much publicity. Although very popular in the past, other vehicles now compete for the investor's attention. Whereas once warrants were one of the most highly leveraged investments, they must now compete with equity options, index options, stock index futures, and options on stock index futures. Nevertheless, some of the characteristics that made them popular in the past still exist. The patient and persevering investor can find worthwhile prospecting in the list of traded warrants. Investments can be uncovered that are attractive in their own right and that can contribute to diversification in a well planned portfolio.

Unfortunately, warrants are complex instruments. Very little information currently exists to assist the investor in analyzing and selecting these securities. They are truly overlooked. The purpose of this book is to supply this missing information. It will answer such questions as:

What is a warrant and how are they created?
What are the sources of information covering warrants?
How are warrants analyzed?
What are the risks and pitfalls of warrant investing?
What unique investment strategies do warrants provide?
What advantages do warrants have over stock options?

The book begins with an overview describing the fundamentals of warrants including a description, history, background, and a brief specification of the instrument. Basic evaluation techniques are then presented. Generally these are simple tools, rules of thumb, and elementary calculations which permit the investor to determine quickly the attractiveness of a particular issue. This is followed by a section covering rigorous analytical techniques, those with theoretical underpinnings.

This material is followed by several sections on investment strategy. Programs are described that are suitable for speculators interested in high risk/high reward situations. Other programs—hedges, in particular—are described which are suitable for conservative, risk averse investors. This is followed by a discussion of related factors such as margin requirements, taxes, and commissions.

The book concludes with appendixes providing information sources, a statistical summary, and a glossary. A thorough bibliography is provided to document research on the subject and to provide a convenient source of information for those wishing to pursue the subject in further detail.

DONALD T. MESLER
Chicago, Illinois

CONTENTS

CHAPTER

1

OVERVIEW

INTRODUCTION

A common stock purchase warrant is an option. As such, most of the theory, nomenclature, and evaluation techniques applicable to options can be used in the analysis of warrants. In the past, warrants have been somewhat of an enigma, truly understood by relatively few individuals. However, exchange trading of puts and calls has brought the concepts of options into the public domain. Therefore the nature of warrants should no longer be foreign.

The literature on warrants is extensive. Most of it, however, is confined to academic publications and texts targeted at graduate students. Little has been presented for public consumption. As a result, most warrant trades are probably executed in ignorance, and thousands of shares are held by individuals and institutions who have little understanding of

the security which they own. At the same time, market forces
are causing distortions in the prices of many of these issues.
Some have reached ridiculously high levels while others are
dirt cheap. Many investors, in possession of the right information, would immediately take appropriate buy or sell ac-
tions on their holdings.

Unfortunately, warrants are complex instruments. They
are, in reality, options, and much of the theory of that discipline applies directly to warrants. Therefore, the typical investor is at a loss to understand and analyze the investment.
The intended function of this book is to assist investors in
reaching buy or sell decisions for warrants in which they
might have an interest.

The assumption is frequently made that if the stock is
attractive, the warrant is automatically more desirable. Such
a conclusion is not necessarily justified. It may be that the
stock is the more attractive investment. An exploration of the
factors which elevate the warrant to preferred status is also a
primary goal of this text.

BACKGROUND AND HISTORY

Common stock purchase warrants are venerable securities.
Unfortunately, however, they have a somewhat checkered
history. First of all, they are a form of option and are therefore
highly speculative. Secondly, during the depression they were
issued in reorganizations of troubled companies. Thus, they
are not traditionally associated with companies of highest
quality. And thirdly, they were an orphaned security. For
most of its history the New York Stock Exchange refused to
permit warrants to be listed. This condition did not change
until the introduction of the American Telephone and
Telegraph warrant in 1974.

The first warrant appeared in 1911, the American Elec-
tric Power warrant. Since that time the list has grown in fits

and starts. At times they have captured a public following while at other times they have fallen into disfavor. The current situation is very positive as will be discussed subsequently.

The popularity of this type of security was never overwhelming, and until the mid-sixties only a few dozen were available. At that time the stock market exhibited a period of great strength. A roaring and speculative bull market was conducive to the issuance of warrants. New equity issues, often with warrants attached, were commonplace. In addition, merger activity was rampant and warrants were often used as part of the takeover package. Also at that time real estate investment trusts had a surge in popularity, and they also made frequent use of warrants. Warrants were awarded a new respectability and they were issued with abandon.

That period was to be the heyday for some time to come. Several devastating bear markets—1969, 1973, 1977, and 1981—ended much of the activity in initial public offerings and in mergers and acquisitions, prime factors in the creation of new warrant issues. The concept of the conglomerate—frequent users of warrants—reached its golden age, and a reversal in that phase of corporate history began. In addition, there was a new game for speculators—listed options, a creation of the Chicago Board Options Exchange.

From the late 1960s until 1982 or 1983 the list of available warrants steadily declined. Even the outstanding bull market which began in 1974 and the accompanying surge in new issues did not trigger much interest in warrants. The issues of earlier years expired one by one, and replacements came only sporadically. The list shrank and those issues which did exist were mostly uninteresting, at least from the perspectives presented in this text. Warrants had once again fallen out of favor.

In the early 1980s, however, a new cycle appears to have begun. Inflation was licked (if only temporarily) and the economy took a major turn upward. In 1982 a bull market of major proportions got underway. It was accompanied by significant moves in both blue chip and secondary stocks. Volume of trading set new records. In this environment activity in mergers and acquisitions resumed. The new issues market boomed.

And guess what? There was a revival of interest in stock purchase warrants. They once again became investment vehicles in widespread use. As a result, the list of publicly traded warrants expanded in the 1983 to 1984 time frame to its longest length ever. As of this writing in 1985 more than 425 different issues compete for the attention of investors.

DEFINITION AND BASIC CHARACTERISTICS

A warrant is an option to buy a security at a specified price for a specified period of time. The optioned security is usually common stock. However, warrants are also available to purchase preferred stock and debt instruments as well. The amount which must be surrendered with each warrant to receive a unit of the optioned security is known as the exercise price. In options terminology this is equivalent to the strike price.

Warrants originate in many ways. Most frequently they accompany new debt or equity offerings because they facilitate the sale while at the same time satisfying needs of the buyer and seller alike. For example, a company issuing bonds usually pays a lower interest rate if warrants are attached to the issue. However, the company is not getting something for nothing since the warrants, like other options, have real value. In addition to their use in underwritings, warrants have been used as dividends to shareholders. They frequently are part of a package of securities proffered in mergers and acquisitions. Finally, warrants often appear in reorganizations or recapitalizations.

Warrants are purchased by investors willing to tolerate high risk in return for potentially high rewards. Warrants can also be used like options in conjunction with other securities to alter the risk reward characteristics of a position. Finally, warrant price movements are intimately tied to another security and aberrations occur in relative pricing. These permit hedging and arbitrage strategies to capitalize on undervalued or overvalued situations.

Warrants have been issued by all types of companies representing a cross section of American industry. They are not restricted to highly speculative companies or those in poor financial condition. Exhibit 1-1 is a tabulation of warrants whose underlying security trades on either the New York Stock Exchange, the American Stock Exchange, or the Pacific Stock Exchange. An even larger number of warrants exists for over-the-counter stocks. Investors with an interest in any of these securities should not take any action until more details of warrant trading have unfolded. Warrant terms are frequently complex, and a special provision might negate an otherwise attractive investment.

THE WARRANT DIAGRAM

The terms of a warrant and certain characteristics of the marketplace partially constrict the range of possible prices. The allowable region—applicable to warrants to purchase one share of common stock for cash—is shown in Exhibit 1-2.

Minimum Value

To acquire stock through an option requires an outlay of both the option price and the exercise price. If the stock is below the exercise price, outright purchase is cheaper than buying an option to exercise. Thus the warrant is worthless and the

---

EXHIBIT 1-1
Listed Stocks for Which Warrants Are Available
(May 1985)

ADI Electronics   Equitec Financial Group
APL Corp.   FPA Corp.
Acton Corp.   Facet Enterprises
Adams Resources & Energy   Frontier Airlines
Alleghany Corp.   Fuqua Industries

Altex Oil   GTI Corp.
American Express Company   GenCorp Inc.
American General Corp.   Genesco
American Pacific International   Geothermal Resources International
American Science & Engineering   Giant Portland-Masonry & Cement

Angeles Corp.   Golden Nugget Inc.
Apache Petroleum   Goldfield Corp.
Atlas Corp.   Grant Industries
BSN Corp.   Grolier Inc.
Bally Manufacturing   Harnischfeger

Beker Industries   Healthamerica Corp.
Beltran Corp.   Heldor Industries
Blair, John & Co.   Helionetics
Caesars World   Horn & Hardart
Calton Inc.   Hotel Properties Inc.

Charter Company   ICN Pharmaceuticals
Collins Foods International   Imperial Industries
Commonwealth Oil Refining   Inco Ltd.
Conquest Exploration Co.   Instrument Systems
Consolidated Oil & Gas   International Banknote

Cosmopolitan Care Corp.   International Harvester
Custom Energy Services   International Thoroughbred
Datametrics   Jet America Air
Digicon, Inc.   Kenai Corp.
Diversified Industries   Keystone Camera Products Corp.

Dome Petroleum Ltd.   Kidde, Inc.
ERC International   Lomas & Nettleton Mortgage Investors
Eastern Airlines   Lundy Electronics & Systems
Electro Audio Dynamics   M.D.C. Corp.
Electronic Memories & Magnetics   MGM/UA Entertainment Co.

EXHIBIT 1-1—*Continued*
Listed Stocks for Which Warrants Are Available
(May 1985)

MSA Realty Corp.
Macrodyne Industries
Massey-Ferguson
Mattel Incorporated
McDermott International

McLean Industries
Mitral Medical International
Mobile Home Industries
Mortgage and Realty Trust
Muse Air Corp.

NCNB Corp.
National Patent Development
Newpark Resources
Nortek Inc.
Nu Horizons Electronics

Oak Industries
Occidental Petroleum
Orion Pictures
Pan Am Corp
Penril Corp.

Petro-Lewis Corp.
Pier 1 Inc.
Public Service Co. of New Hampshire
Republic Airlines

Rooney Pace Group

Safeguard Scientifics
Spendthrift Farm
Standard Havens
Storage Equities
Storer Communications

Sunshine Mining Co.
Texas International Co.
Tiger International
Total Petroleum (NA)
Transworld Corp.

Tri-Continental Corp.
Triangle Industries
Triton Energy
Tyler Corp.
USAir Group

US Home Corp
Warner Communications
Webb (Del E.)
Western Air Lines
Wickes Companies, Inc.

Willcox & Gibbs
Winners Corp.

minimum value is zero. If the stock is above the exercise price the warrant minimum value is the amount which, when added to the exercise price, just equals the stock price. In other words, the warrant minimum value is the difference between the stock price and the exercise price. The minimum value is also known as the intrinsic value.

EXHIBIT 1–2
Zone of Plausible Warrant Prices

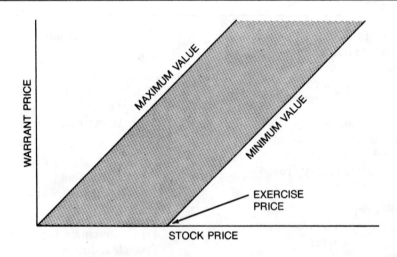

Maximum Value

A rational investor would not pay more for the option to buy a security than would be paid for the security itself. Thus, for any given stock price, the maximum value the warrant can assume is that stock price.

In theory, warrants should trade somewhere between the two extremes of minimum and maximum value, and this is confirmed by real world observations. As a function of the common stock price the warrant price has a smooth curved trajectory or track as shown in Exhibit 1-3.

When the stock is zero the warrant is worthless. As the stock increases in value so does the option to buy the stock. In addition, the warrant assumes a speculative value over and above its intrinsic value known as *premium*. The maximum premium occurs when the stock price equals the exercise price. For higher stock prices the warrant price will continue to increase, but the premium will diminish reaching zero when the common stock sells at about three to five times the exercise price.

EXHIBIT 1-3
Relationship of a Warrant Price to the Price of its Underlying Common Stock

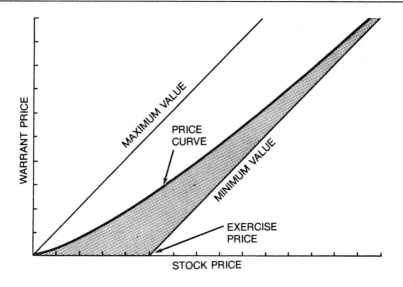

Normal Value Curve

There is no simple model for determining a warrant's price. Attempts at finding a precise mathematical statement have been unsuccessful; in fact, it is unlikely that such a mathematical solution exists.

A curve satisfactory for making investment decisions has been derived from option theory, simple mathematics, and historical evidence. This curve is given in Exhibit 1-4 and is applicable for long-term warrants on volatile non-dividend paying stocks. In this graph both the stock price and the warrant price have been normalized; that is, the vertical axis represents the stock price divided by the exercise price and the horizontal axis represents the stock price divided by the exercise price. By using normalized prices warrants having different exercise prices can be plotted on a single graph for comparison. Per share (adjusted) warrant prices must be

EXHIBIT 1–4
Warrant Normal Value Curve

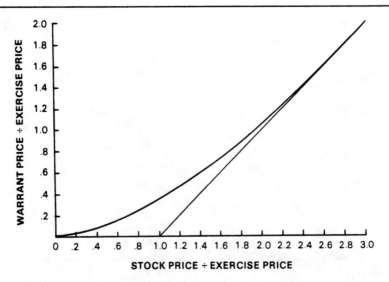

calculated before using the chart. The adjusted price equals
the traded price divided by the conversion ratio. The conversion ratio is the number of shares of the underlying security
for which the warrant can be exchanged.

The exact model from which this curve is derived is discussed in Chapter 6. Modifications to the curve necessary to
reflect all the parameters which affect a warrant's price are
also discussed there.

COMPARISON WITH OPTIONS

Warrants have many similarities with call options. However,
there are also a few important basic differences.

Warrants are generally issued by the corporation whose
stock the warrant is a privilege to buy. Frequently this is not

stock already in existence and requires a new stock issue. Options, on the other hand, are an agreement between two parties to buy and sell. Existing shares change hands if the option is exercised.

Exercise of warrants increases the number of shares of corporate stock outstanding. Therefore, exercise means that the firm's assets and profits are spread over a larger number of shares; that is, dilution occurs. In contrast, call options do not change the corporate capital structure. There is no dilution.

When a warrant is offered, the size of the issue is fixed. Subsequent to that time the only likely change is a decrease in the issue size caused by exercise of the warrants. The number of options outstanding for a particular issue is unpredictable and may increase or decrease erratically, depending upon the number of buyers and sellers able to meet and agree on terms.

The final important difference between calls and warrants is the lifetime of the option. Exchange-traded options have a maximum life of nine months. In contrast, warrants appear having a variety of life spans generally measured in years (typically five to ten). Some are even longer and a few are perpetual; that is, they never expire.

THE WARRANT AGREEMENT

The terms of a warrant are spelled out in the prospectus or offering circular accompanying the issue. Another source of such information is the annual report of the company which issued the warrant. The warrant is usually described in the section labeled "Capital Shares" in the Notes to Consolidated Financial Statements.

Advisory services and annual reports generally provide quantitative data only—information such as the exercise price, expiration date, and number of shares outstanding. For more complete numerical information and for most qualitative information—such as what happens to the warrants in the event of mergers, takeovers, or bankruptcy—the investor must turn to the warrant agreement.

The warrant agreement is a document much like a bond indenture. It contains all the terms, provisions, and exceptions specific to a particular warrant issue in addition to the warrant holder's rights under a variety of circumstances. The warrant agreement is available to investors on request from the treasurer's office of the issuing company or from shareholder relations. Frequently a telephone call produces the document by mail within a short time. If the warrant agreement does not arrive promptly it may be because the request is unusual and the clerk processing the request is unfamiliar with the document. However, persistence generally produces the desired result.

Even the warrant agreement is not the last word on the matter. Over the years cases have been documented where the company did not act to comply with the terms and intent of the warrant agreement often resulting in legal action and, unfortunately, often resulting in a breach of the warrant holder's rights. Most of the cases are now old history, but the warrant market has also been rather dull for many years. Whether or not these shenanigans will again resume now that the warrant market has once again come alive is open to conjecture.

Nevertheless, the warrant agreement is the definitive source of a warrant's terms and provisions. Warrant holders, especially those holding large numbers of shares, are well advised to obtain a copy of this document and to study it carefully.

CHAPTER

2

THE ISSUER'S PERSPECTIVE

INTRODUCTION

Warrants originate in many ways. Most frequently they accompany new debt or equity offerings because they facilitate the sale while at the same time satisfying particular needs of buyer and seller alike. For example, a company issuing bonds usually pays a lower interest rate if warrants are attached to the issue. However, the company is not getting something for nothing since the warrants, like other options, have real value.

There are many misconceptions about why a warrant (or for that matter, any convertible security) is issued. Most writers describe warrants as "sweeteners" or "kickers." Unfortunately, the theory of finance states that there is no justifi-

13

cation for any securities other than debt and equity. This would include warrants, preferred stock, convertible bonds, convertible preferred stock, and any other vehicle which clever financiers may design.

WHY ARE WARRANTS ISSUED?

The need to finance triggers the question of how to finance. Of course, there are a myriad of alternatives. What is the decision making process which causes warrants to be chosen in lieu of conventional debt or equity issues or more exotic securities such as convertibles?

Unfortunately, the answer to this question is neither simple nor obvious. Many commentators dismiss the matter rather quickly. Warrants are categorized as "sweeteners" or "kickers" included in the financing package to obtain more favorable terms for the issuer. Not only is this description incorrect, but it also flies in the face of common sense when considered realistically.

FUNDAMENTAL CONCEPTS FROM THE THEORY OF FINANCE

A firm is an accumulation of assets which, in conjunction with the cash flows which they produce, establish the overall value of the organization. The firm has numerous financing alternatives, the mix of different securities being known as its capital structure.

When the firm is financed entirely by common stock, all the cash flows accrue to the stockholders. When debt is issued in addition to equity securities, the cash flow is divided in two parts. Debt holders have a relatively assured claim on the cash flows while the stockholders have a claim which is less certain—in other words, more risky. Other classes of securities in the capital structure could be described similarly.

From the myriad of alternatives available to the financier it would seem obvious that the optimum choice of security to issue would be that which maximized the overall value of the firm. Unfortunately, modern financial theory states that a firm cannot change the total value of its securities just by splitting its cash flows into different streams. The value of the firm is determined by its real assets, not by the securities it issues. Thus, capital structure is irrelevant.

This bold conclusion is precise only in the ideal case of perfect capital markets (PCM). The conditions for PCM are as follows:

1.   No transaction costs,
2.   Free information readily available, and
3.   Zero taxes.

However, researchers have examined the basic proposition—that is, the irrelevance of capital structure—with PCM conditions relaxed. While difficult to prove rigorously, the basic premise nevertheless has been found to describe reality.

Increasing the value of a firm through changes in the capital structure is still a possibility for an astute financier. The task is to design a unique and desirable instrument that satisfies a demand previously incapable of being filled. It is unlikely, however, that this instrument will be anything like conventional debt and equity. Even warrants are so commonplace that they fail to qualify for this task.

"KICKERS" AND "SWEETENERS": TERMS TO AVOID

The message of this section is straightforward: the terms "kicker" and "sweetener" are misnomers in the context of warrant financing. Investors and analysts should delete these terms from their vocabulary when addressing warrant-related subjects.

Bonds which are otherwise equivalent can generally be floated at a lower interest rate when warrants are attached. A warrant is frequently referred to as a "sweetener" to explain this fact. Warrants do induce lenders to make funds available to borrowers at lower interest rates than would otherwise be the case. This observation, however, seems to imply that some great benefit is received at little or no cost. However, as in all matters relating to Wall Street, the principle that "there is no free lunch" applies with equal certainty to warrant investors.

The central point of this argument is as follows. Warrants are options and have value, often substantial. Management has no authority to issue stock options without full consideration. The interest saved by having a lower bond coupon is matched by the actual cost of the warrant to the issuer. In the long run, the issuer is neither ahead nor behind no matter which strategy is elected—high coupon bonds without warrants or low coupon bonds with warrants.

VALID JUSTIFICATIONS

There are two exceptions to this general rule. First, companies may have cash flow problems. Even though the two alternatives may be equivalent—high yielding bonds or low yielding bonds with warrants attached—the company may prefer the low yield approach so that cash is available for other uses rather than being paid out as interest. The second reason companies may wish to issue a variety of securities is that shareholders tend to be loyal. By having various forms of debt and equity, securities of every risk class are available which appeal to a broad spectrum of investors.

The lender should also be ambivalent about the terms of the debt. High interest loans without warrants or low interest loans with warrants should be equally attractive. Realistically, however, one practical aspect may make the bond-warrants combination more appealing. Assume that the debt is subordinated. The company may issue additional senior bonds, placing the holder of the subordinated debt in a riskier position. The inclusion of a warrant feature guarantees a piece of the action even though other circumstances may be detrimental.

WARRANT FINANCING PACKAGES

Academics can debate the need for warrants and question their use as the optimal financing vehicle. Nevertheless the popularity of warrants is at an all-time high. Issuers seem convinced of their usefulness and not just in limited situations. The following is a discussion of the various ways in which warrants have been used in successful financing ventures.

Attached to Senior Securities

Warrants often appear as part of a unit in conjunction with a straight debt issue. Usually they can be detached, and a separate market develops for the warrants, for the bonds with the warrants attached, and for the bonds ex-warrants. This form of financing is probably the most frequently deployed use of warrants.

Accompanying Common Stock Issues

Warrants accompanying common stock are the second most popular form of warrant financing. In the new issues market such packages are seen frequently. However, established companies tapping the equity markets frequently utilize the warrant as well.

Dividends to Shareholders

Warrants have been used to compensate shareholders in lieu of cash dividends or stock dividends. Although the recipients generally do not understand or appreciate such a distribution, it can be an astute business transaction for the issuer.

Such warrants inevitably are listed and an active market develops with prices determined by free market forces. Having thus established a value for their warrant, the issuer can look forward to using additional warrants for other purposes, perhaps in conjunction with acquisitions and mergers.

Compensation in Mergers and Acquisitions

The securities exchanged for the assets of a takeover target include virtually all available types. Although not the most popular of instruments used for this purpose, warrants are used occasionally. With merger activity currently in an active phase and with warrants having a resurgence of popularity, their use in corporate combinations may be anticipated to increase.

Direct Sale to the Public and/or Shareholders

Although this transaction has been successfully implemented, it is not utilized frequently. An explanation is not readily forthcoming, especially in view of the popularity of the bond/warrant and stock/warrant units. No doubt it is the warrant's complexity and public ignorance of its features which limit this type of financing.

Compensation in Reorganizations

Warrants are issued from time to time to stockholders of failed corporations. They may have seen their equity erode to nil in the course of the deterioration of their company, the creditors having a claim on all that remains. The warrants are often a compromise with the company's creditors. They permit the shareholder to retain an equity interest at minimal cost to the surviving company. When financial assistance is required—such as an injection of capital—lenders are often more lenient in the terms (such as interest payments) if they receive warrants as part of the package.

Compensation to Underwriters

Careful perusal of prospectuses, in particular those for new issues of start-up companies, often reveals that warrants have been used extensively in the process of making the public offering. Undercapitalized entrepreneurs do not have idle cash and require the entire proceeds from the successful sale of a new issue to finance their objectives. Underwriters often accept warrants as one component of their compensation. These warrants are usually restricted securities. Disposition by the underwriter is often difficult or impossible, and a public market seldom develops.

The number of warrants which underwriters receive often defies rational explanation. Nevertheless, these warrants provide a powerful incentive to complete a successful underwriting and to nurture the underlying stock so that it performs well in the aftermarket. In a well executed deal such warrants have a trivial cost basis and, in the right environment, can be sold or exercised at some future date with long term capital gains and favorable tax consequences.

CHAPTER
3

THE INVESTOR'S PERSPECTIVE

INTRODUCTION

The investor's perspective is slightly more complicated than might initially be imagined. This is because warrants are complex instruments, and investments using warrants assume many forms. Warrants are highly leveraged making them an excellent choice for speculating in the market. Being options, their price is driven by the underlying issue. The stock versus warrant price relationship is quite predictable and, when it is out of line, various hedging and arbitrage opportunities present themselves. Finally, warrants can be treated as an alternative to the underlying common, a true substitute investment. The question as to which is more appropriate—the stock or the warrant—is not necessarily easy

to answer. This problem will be addressed in complete detail
in Chapter 5.

ATTRIBUTES AND SHORTCOMINGS

An investor with a good record at selecting stocks will find
the highly leveraged warrant to be a most attractive alternative. Other investors who will find warrants attractive are
those who take the time to ferret out issues which are mispriced; that is, selling for more or less than might be expected
under the circumstances.

There are problems associated with warrant investing,
however. First of all a great deal of work is involved. A
specialized body of knowledge is required to analyze these
instruments. Generally this information is not readily available, and the investor is therefore obligated to purchase rather
expensive advisory services. Because only a few issues are
attractive at any particular juncture, a considerable amount
of time must be devoted to studying the statistics. For more
sophisticated investors, experimenting with securities in various combinations until a desirable risk/reward posture can
be obtained will require even more time.

Once the investment is selected new problems arise. Usually the strategies are foreign to the investor's stockbroker.
Rules about margin and short sales will most likely have to be
explained in detail. Also the broker will have to be directed
carefully when executing the transactions as they are not
routine, especially when hedging is attempted.

Trading in warrants is prone to a number of nasty pitfalls.
They are wasting assets so they cannot be purchased and
forgotten about as can many other securities. Also, warrants
frequently have special terms which become activated at a
future date. Since these often have an adverse impact on the
warrant's price they should be anticipated well in advance.

Another source of risk arises in takeover situations. Frequently, warrant holders are not compensated fairly. The possibility of mergers and acquisitions must be given serious consideration and if these occur in a warrant in which an investor has a position, additional time will be required to follow the news and develop the best strategy for handling the situation.

Finally, warrant terms are not quite as definite as various documents and exchange procedures might indicate. This is especially true regarding the expiration date. In the past certain warrants have been extended without proper justification for this process in the warrant agreement and apparently in violation of exchange procedures. Investors who are short these warrants with the expectation that they will expire worthless will find carefully analyzed situations in complete disarray.

MISPRICED WARRANTS

One goal of any investment strategy is the identification of undervalued and overvalued situations. A consistent program involving purchase and sale of such issues should allow an investor to outperform the market over the long term. Since the warrant's value is inextricably tied to the stock price, locating aberrations in the warrant versus stock price relationship is an excellent means of identifying mispriced warrants.

Why might warrants become underpriced or overpriced? One answer is that warrants are not scrutinized with the intensity necessary to cause efficient pricing. They are ignored by many institutions, for example, because charters forbid inclusion of warrants in their portfolios or because warrant positions cannot be accumulated in sufficient quantity to build worthwhile positions.

There are many circumstances which might cause failure

of warrant prices to track stock prices predictably. A large
upswing or downswing in the common is occasionally
greeted by a much more leisurely move in the warrant. It is
possible to capitalize on these situations since the unusual
relationships often exist for extended periods.

Warrants are also influenced by different supply and demand factors than the common stock. For example, as was
stated earlier, certain institutions cannot or will not hold
warrant positions. Nevertheless they may acquire a position
unintentionally as would be the case if a stock they own
declares a warrant dividend. The disposal of these warrants
sometimes causes tremendous selling pressure not reflected
in the price of the common. Once again, an alert investor can
capitalize on these situations.

INVESTMENT STRATEGIES

Although highly leveraged, in many cases marginable, and
frequently options on second tier companies, warrants need
not be speculative securities. Of course, if speculation is the
objective, the warrant may be the ideal vehicle. But other
strategies, hedges in particular, are also potentially attractive.
The possibility of high returns can be retained while the
exposure to loss is greatly curtailed.

Speculating

The attractiveness of warrants for speculation is self-evident.
They are highly leveraged and often marginable. They are
available for many less-than-blue-chip stocks, exactly those
issues which have the greatest likelihood of making major
moves. Speculators will not generally find listed options on
these stocks, and warrants are an ideal substitute. Chapter 7 is
devoted exclusively to the use of warrants as a speculative
vehicle.

Warrant Hedging

Locating undervalued or overvalued warrants is not necessarily the complete answer to an investment problem. Warrants are volatile securities, and the risk in establishing positions (either long or short) is extremely high—usually higher than most investors are willing to entertain. As with other investments, however, this risk can be modified by combining the warrant position with an offsetting position in a related security. Such a combination is called a hedge, and there are two primary types, the convertible hedge and the reverse hedge.

Convertible Hedges

The lesser known of the two strategies—but equally as powerful—is to purchase undervalued warrants and sell options, stock, or other related securities. The objective is to capitalize on a mispriced security while maintaining control of risk with the short position. Grossly undervalued warrants do not occur frequently, but they are available with sufficient regularity that the list is worth monitoring continually. Chapter 8 is devoted exclusively to convertible hedges.

Reverse Warrant Hedges

This strategy, the most popular because it has received the attention of several financial writers, involves the short sale of overpriced expiring warrants combined with the purchase of the underlying common stock. The warrant is a wasting asset, and this hedge captures the premium while at the same time providing a wide band in which the stock can trade without causing a loss in the position. Reverse warrant hedging is, for all practical purposes, the same as covered call writing or variable call writing. Chapter 9 is devoted exclusively to reverse hedges.

STOCK VERSUS WARRANT

It is generally believed that warrants enable investors to get more bang for the buck. An investor uncovers an interesting situation, and his broker then advises of the existence of a warrant. Since everyone knows that the warrant possesses leverage, the decision to purchase the warrant in lieu of the stock is made without additional evidence. Depending upon the warrant's parameters, this may or may not be a good decision but generally it cannot be made in such a haphazard manner. The stock versus warrant decision is a rather difficult one. It entails calculations requiring a sophisticated understanding of warrant price behavior and its characteristics as a wasting asset. This matter is addressed in further detail in Chapter 5.

CHAPTER
4

DETERMINANTS OF WARRANT PRICES

INTRODUCTION

In previous chapters we have considered the warrant diagram and the constraints which place a minimum and maximum value on a warrant. In practice the warrant will settle in at a price level somewhere between the two extremes. In this chapter we will examine the various factors which influence a warrant's ultimate price. The initial focus will be on theoretical considerations—those arising from option theory and pricing models. After these matters are resolved, the discussion will turn to other factors affecting a warrant's price; namely, the terms and special features provided for in the warrant agreement.

It should be stressed again that even though the factors which influence a warrant's price have been identified and in

27

many cases quantified, the warrant leads an independent life.
All other factors unchanged, every time the stock trades at a
given price the warrant price is not consistent. Although
strongly influenced by certain factors, warrants can be cheap
or dear in comparison to previous warrant prices at the same
stock price. More specifically, the warrant market is ineffi-
cient, and price does not always reflect value. This circum-
stance is fortunate because, as will be demonstrated in later
chapters, techniques are available to capitalize on erratic
warrant price behavior.

THEORETICAL CONSIDERATIONS

A warrant is an option and, generally speaking, all the find-
ings of option theorists can be applied directly to warrants.
The elements which affect a warrant's price (or more impor-
tantly, its premium) as identified by option theorists are as
follows:

1. The relationship of the stock price to the exercise price,
2. The volatility of the underlying instrument,
3. The remaining life,
4. The stock dividend, and
5. The prevailing interest rate.

Other factors have been investigated to ascertain their
effect on a warrant's premium. The research, however, is not
conclusive. These factors include:

1. Whether or not the warrant has an exchange listing,
2. Availability of listed options,
3. Recent price history of the common stock, and
4. Potential dilution of the common stock.

Relationship of the Stock Price to the Exercise Price

The warrant premium over intrinsic value is highest when the stock price is at the exercise price. When the warrant is well out-of-the money there is a low probability that it will ever be exercised. This fact is reflected in very low premiums. When the warrant is well in-the-money the leverage disappears and on a percentage basis warrant price changes resemble those of the underlying common stock. The warrant possesses no advantage, and this is reflected once again in low premiums.

Stock Volatility

The greater the volatility of the underlying stock the higher the warrant's premium. Inherent in volatile stocks is the greatest potential for a large price upswing during the life of the warrant.

Time Until Expiration

The longer the life of the warrant, the higher the premium. Warrant holders wager that the underlying stock will advance sufficiently during the warrant's life that they can benefit from the warrant's great leverage. The shorter the warrant's life the less the likelihood that the leverage will be operative and the less premium the buyer will be willing to pay.

Stock Dividend

The higher the yield on the common stock the lower will be the warrant premium. When high dividends are paid the stock becomes increasingly attractive vis-à-vis the warrant. Also, high dividends are usually associated with mature companies. It is in growth companies that a warrant's leverage is likely to pay off.

Prevailing Interest Rate

The higher interest rates are, in general, the higher the warrant premium. A warrant owner has the equivalent of a position in the underlying stock at a fraction of the investment—similar to buying on installment credit. This delayed payment feature is more and more valuable as interest rates climb.

WARRANT TERMS AND SPECIFICATIONS

There are only four terms which the designers of a warrant issue can make variable; the conversion ratio, the exercise price, the duration, and the dilution protection. Of these, no examples of changing dilution protection (which will be explained subsequently) have ever surfaced. The variations on the other elements in the equation are, however, numerous. There are provisions for increasing warrant life, decreasing warrant life, increasing the exercise price, decreasing the exercise price, and retiring the issue prematurely. Some warrants have had features which are equivalent to an attached put option. An example will be illustrated in Chapter 7.

Incorporating these provisions is not an arbitrary matter. In some instances, such as the put feature of The Charter Company warrant, the issue is made more desirable to a specific group of investors. More often, however, the terms serve the issuer's interests. They permit the company to alter its capitalization under certain circumstances.

Comprehensive warrant statistics complete with footnotes are given in Appendix B. However, to give some indication as to the complexity of the provisions and the extent to which they are employed, the following examples are provided.

Senior Securities Usable at Par

When warrants are issued with bonds there is frequently a provision that the bond can be used at par value as a substitute for cash when exercising the warrant. If the bond is selling above par this feature is of no consequence as it is more economical to use cash for the exercise price. However, if the bond is selling below par the bond should be purchased at a discount and used at full face value in lieu of cash.

Exercising a warrant with a bond valued at par but purchased at a discount from par is equivalent to obtaining a like discount in the exercise price. This feature, which is generally reflected in the market price of the warrant, adds another element of uncertainty to warrant analysis since the discount in the exercise price will increase or decrease as the bond advances or declines. Additional insights into usable bonds are presented in Chapter 11.

Example: McDermott International Warrants. Straight bonds—the 10s of 2003—are usable at par value in lieu of cash when exercising the warrants. There are also other special provisions which apply to this warrant and they will be discussed subsequently.

Call Provisions

A common feature is the call provision. The warrant is callable or redeemable by the issuer at a specified price. There is usually a qualifier; that is, the warrant cannot be called until after a preset date or until the common has traded at a particular price for a specified period of time.

The purpose of the call provision is to force conversion of the warrants. Usually a warrant is called only when it is in-the-money and when its intrinsic value exceeds the call price. Warrant holders must then exercise or suffer a loss equal to the difference between the intrinsic value and the call price.

If a usable bond is involved and that bond is trading below par, it will be utilized in the exercise process. Thus by calling the warrant, the issuer can sometimes cause significant changes in the company's capitalization.

Example: Western Air Lines Warrants.   These warrants are callable at $3 after June 14, 1986 if the common closes at or above $11.875 for 30 consecutive days.

Extension Provisions

Many warrant agreements confer the right on the issuer to extend the life of a warrant. Some permit one extension. Some warrant agreements permit several extensions.
Extensions generally—but not always—occur when the warrant is out of the money and likely to expire worthless. Corporate cash requirements may make it preferable to give the warrant new life rather than to permit its demise.

Example: International Harvester Warrants.   The company reserves the right to extend the expiration date from December 15, 1993 to December 15, 1999.

Exercise Price Changes

Certain warrant agreements schedule periodic changes in the exercise price of the warrant over the life of the issue. Interestingly, these may be step-ups in the exercise price or reductions in the exercise price. A reduction in the exercise price may put the warrant in-the-money and thus make exercise an attractive alternative for warrant holders. Increases in the exercise price are designed to keep returns to warrant holders commensurate with those of common shareholders. Presumably the resulting decrease in warrant value is incorporated in a formula for the anticipated growth rate of the underlying common.

Example: McDermott International Warrants. The company has the right to reduce the exercise price by one third at any time.

Acceleration Provisions

A few warrants have the provision that the expiration date can be accelerated, often contingent upon a particular price for the underlying stock. Accelerating the maturity of an in-the-money warrant is another means of forcing conversion.

Example: McDermott International Warrants. The company can accelerate the expiration date to April 1, 1988 from April 1, 1990 if the common is a least 125 percent of the exercise price for 20 days within a 30 consecutive trading day period.

Put Provisions

Occasionally the issuer adds terms which enable holders to return the warrant to the issuer for consideration. This is, in essence, a built-in put option. The feature provides a floor for the warrant and, of course, distorts the normal value curve on the lower portion of its trajectory.

Example: Charter Company Warrants. The Charter Company warrant has had an interesting history. Its price has been extremely volatile, and the warrant was selected for further analysis in speculative strategies covered in Chapter 7. Unfortunately, however, the company filed for Chapter XI bankruptcy proceedings on April 20, 1984, and the warrant provisions are now meaningless. The put provision stated that the warrant could be exchanged for $1.25 during ten trading days prior to September 1, 1988 unless already expired.

Dilution Protection

In many instances, warrant holders have made a significant capital contribution to the company in question. If the underlying stock splits or if a special dividend is declared, warrant holders should be entitled to the same consideration as the stockholders. This fact has not gone unnoticed by the financial community, and today virtually all warrants have dilution protection; that is, the warrant terms are adjusted so that warrant holders benefit from all the advantages bestowed upon common shareholders.

CHAPTER
5

BASIC EVALUATION
TECHNIQUES

INTRODUCTION

Warrant analysts have developed a number of tools and
evaluation techniques to determine which warrants are best
situated for purchase or sale and, more specifically, which are
undervalued or overvalued. These tools range from simple
rules of thumb and ratio analyses to sophisticated mathematical models. While it is the elaborate models which are ultimately the most valuable, the simpler tools should not be
overlooked. A study of the simple tools is worthwhile because
they give great insight into a warrant's price behavior. They
are also surprisingly useful. In addition they are the ones
generally cited by analysts and investment advisory services
recommending various strategies, and therefore they should
be understood even though a more sophisticated analysis is

intended. The basic tools will be the exclusive domain of this chapter. The more sophisticated tools and models will be covered in Chapter 6.

An interesting aside to the warrant selection problem presents itself to the investor interested in a particular *stock* and who subsequently learns of the existence of a *warrant* for that particular issue. Should the investor buy the stock or the warrant? The analyses which are included in this chapter will enable the investor to answer this question.

HYPOTHETICAL EXAMPLE

The reader is alerted in advance that no warrant transaction can be justified by the results of a single indicator. All are useful, however, in converging on a buy-hold-sell decision. The tools to be covered in this chapter include the following:

1. Premium,
2. Leverage Indicator,
3. Leverage Ratio,
4. Mathematical Advantage, and
5. Appreciation Multiple.

Accompanying the description of each indicator is a graph to show changes in behavior as the stock moves from below the exercise price to well above the exercise price. The initial discussions involve an undervalued warrant having specified terms; in particular, the exercise price equals 20, the conversion ratio is one, and the remaining life is four years. The following table shows price projections for this warrant at three different stock prices. Procedures for making these projections will be described in Chapter 6.

Stock Price:	10	20	40
Warrant Price:	$1\frac{3}{4}$	6	$20\frac{1}{2}$

The chapter concludes with a summary of the indicators showing how they vary for undervalued warrants, fairly valued warrants, and overvalued warrants. The restrictions caused by specifying the terms are relaxed so that the indicators are easily interpreted for any warrant.

LEVERAGE

Virtually all warrants exhibit some degree of leverage; that is, on a percentage basis they increase in value more than the underlying stock when the stock price advances, and they decrease in value more than the underlying stock when the stock price declines. The leverage results from the fact that the warrant is a proxy for stock ownership but payment for the stock is not required in full; specifically, payment of the exercise price is deferred until some future date.

The ideal warrant would be priced such that it was located in the *corner* of the warrant diagram; that is, the stock price would be at the exercise price and the warrant would have zero premium. Under such circumstances the warrant would advance point for point with the underlying stock but would be immune to stock price declines. The leverage would be high on the upside and negligible on the downside. Of course, such bargains rarely, if ever, exist. As the warrant moves away from the corner the leverage becomes less and less favorable endowing the warrant with varying degrees of attractiveness. The function of the various warrant indicators is to establish a measure of "goodness"—a figure of merit, if you will—as the warrant meanders about the warrant diagram.

Because the warrant price is a complex function of a number of factors, it is unreasonable to expect that a simple ratio or algebraic expression can incorporate enough information to describe the warrant accurately. However, the simple tools can be useful as screening devices to eliminate obviously undesirable issues from further consideration and to target the issues most likely to possess extraordinary investment potential. Once again, no warrant transaction should be initiated based upon signals provided by a single indicator.

PREMIUM CONCEPTS

As discussed in the preceding chapter, warrants generally do not trade at their intrinsic values because they have leverage and investors are willing to pay a price over and above intrinsic value for this leverage feature. The excess of a warrant's market value over its intrinsic value is known as premium. Expressed as a dollar amount this number is not particularly enlightening. However, when expressed as a percentage of the price of the underlying stock, the premium becomes a useful indicator for comparing warrants.

This definition can be stated in equation form. To simplify the presentation we will assume that the security obtainable upon exercise is common stock:

$$\text{Premium} = \frac{\text{warrant market price} - \text{tangible value}}{\text{market value of security obtainable upon exercise}}$$

Using notation:

$$P = \frac{W - (S - E)}{S}$$

$$P = \frac{W - S + E}{S} \tag{5-1}$$

where   P = premium
        E = exercise price
        S = stock price
        W = warrant price

Although the concept of premium is simple, the above equation does not tell the whole story. The value of premium depends on the method selected for calculating intrinsic value. To understand the problem consider once again the warrant diagram shown in Exhibit 5-1. The arrow at point A

EXHIBIT 5-1
Warrant Premium Measures

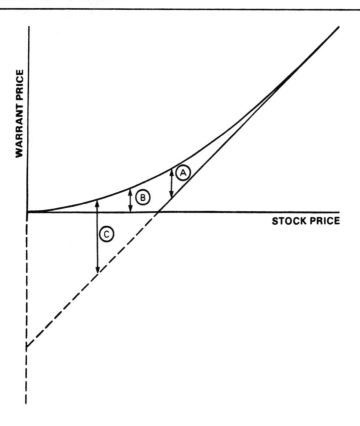

indicates the quantity being measured and the calculation is
straightforward. When the stock is below the exercise price,
however, the premium can be calculated in two different
ways as shown by arrow B and arrow C. The premium as
measured by arrow B does not recognize negative tangible
values while the premium as measured by arrow C does
permit the warrant to assume negative tangible value.

Thus, for stocks trading below the warrant exercise price
two different premium calculations are possible. Furthermore
both have merit and both are in widespread use. Before continuing this discussion we will redefine premium as follows:

$$P1 = \frac{W}{S} \times 100 \; ; S \leqq E \tag{5-2}$$

$$\left.\begin{array}{l}\end{array}\right\}$$ Warrant cannot assume negative tangible value

$$P1 = \frac{W - S + E}{S} \times 100; S > E \tag{5-3}$$

$$P2 = \frac{W - S + E}{S} \times 100; \text{all } S \tag{5-4}$$

$$\left.\begin{array}{l}\end{array}\right\}$$ Warrant can assume negative tangible value

Note that when the stock price equals or exceeds the exercise price the values of P1 and P2 are identical.

The behavior of P1 and P2 is shown graphically in Exhibit 5–2. Figure 1 is the price curve for the warrant under consideration. Figure 2 shows the variation for P1 (warrant negative

---

EXHIBIT 5–2
Premium P1 and P2

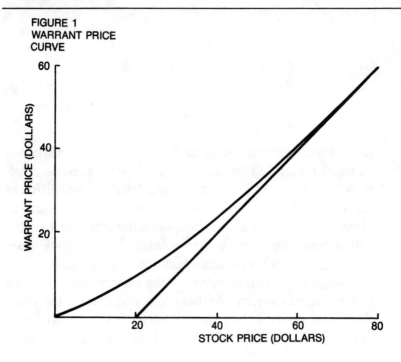

FIGURE 1
WARRANT PRICE
CURVE

EXHIBIT 5-2—*Continued*
Premium P1 and P2

FIGURE 2
PREMIUM P1

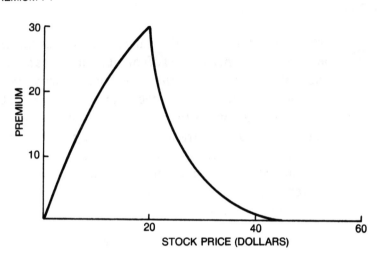

FIGURE 3
PREMIUM P2

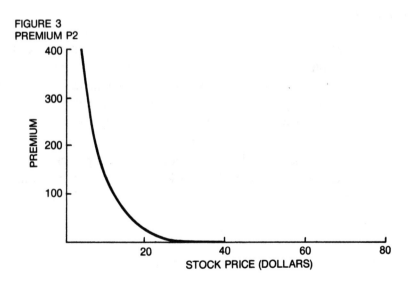

intrinsic value disallowed) for a broad range of stock prices, and Figure 3 is a graph of P2 (warrant negative value permitted) over the same range of stock prices.

Premium (P1)

Premium P1 implies that the warrant cannot assume negative tangible value. This method of calculation relates the warrant price solely to the price of the underlying security. As a result the option premium can never exceed 100 percent. This makes comparisons of the premiums more manageable and more meaningful for trading purposes and is the premium generally encountered in statistical surveys.

Using data from the hypothetical example presented earlier (exercise price equals 20, stock price equals 10, and warrant price equals 1 3/4) the calculation for P1 is as follows:

$$P1 = \frac{1.75}{10} \times 100 = 18\%$$

Premium (P2)

Premium P2 implies that the warrant can assume negative tangible value. It is accurate in that it indicates the percentage advance required of the common to make the warrant's tangible value equal to its current price. However, the high premiums resulting for warrants with stocks well below the exercise price may obscure the attractiveness of such issues.

Using data for the hypothetical warrant presented earlier (exercise price equals 20, stock price equals 10 and warrant price equals 1 3/4) the calculation for P2 is as follows:

$$P2 = \frac{1.75 - 10 + 20}{10} \times 100 = 118\%$$

THE LEVERAGE INDICATOR (LI)

The intent of the leverage indicator is to predict the change which will occur in the price of a warrant given a stated change in the price of the underlying stock. The leverage indicator is one of the simplest of the basic tools but also one of the most useful. The leverage indicator is defined as the price of the optioned stock divided by the price on one share. Symbolically:

$$LI = \frac{S}{W} \qquad (5\text{--}5)$$

Conceptually, the leverage indicator is nothing more than that portion of the current stock price represented by warrant ownership.

If the warrant traded without premium, the leverage indicator would be an outstanding analytical tool with complete accuracy. Assume a hypothetical case where $S/E = 2$ and $W/E = 1$. The leverage indicator therefore equals S/W or 2. Assume the stock increases 25 percent to 2. Therefore the warrant would increase to 1.5, a gain of 50 percent. Comparing the change in warrant price for the change in stock verifies the definition of the leverage indicator:

$$\frac{\Delta W^{1}}{\Delta S} = 2$$

Because warrants do trade with premium, the leverage indicator does not give a precise estimate of the warrant's leverage. Nevertheless it is useful as a first approximation to a warrant's attractiveness.

The general behavior of the leverage indicator is shown in Exhibit 5–3. Figure 1 is the price curve for the warrant under consideration. Figure 2 shows the curves for the leverage indicator assuming that:

1. The warrant trades only at intrinsic value and

2. The warrant trades with premium over a broad range of stock prices.

---

[1] The symbol Δ is the Greek letter delta. In mathematics Δ has been adopted as the symbol signifying change. Thus, ΔW means the change in W.

EXHIBIT 5–3
The Leverage Indicator (LI)

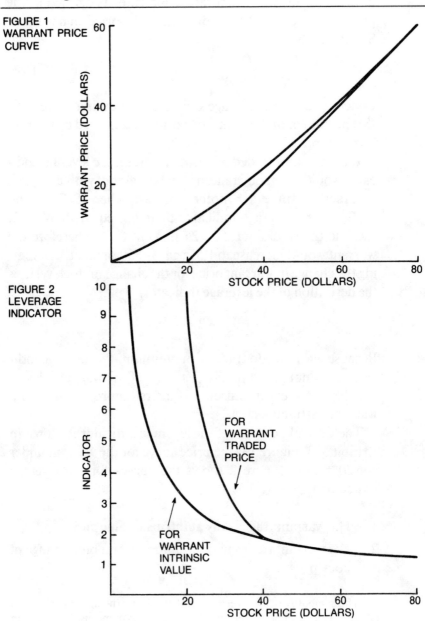

FIGURE 1
WARRANT PRICE
CURVE

FIGURE 2
LEVERAGE
INDICATOR

Using data from the hypothetical example presented earlier (exercise price equals 20, stock price equals 10, and warrant price equals 1 3/4) the calculation of the leverage indicator is as follows:

$$LI = \frac{20}{6}$$

$$LI = 3.33$$

THE LEVERAGE RATIO (LR)

Another approach to measuring leverage is to calculate the percentage change in the price of a warrant resulting from a change (either fixed or variable) in the price of the underlying stock. The calculation is usually performed assuming a doubling (100 percent change) in the price of the underlying stock, and that approach is used in this text.

More specifically, the leverage ratio is defined as:

$$LR = \frac{\frac{W_U - W}{W}}{\frac{S_U - S}{S}}$$

$$LR = \frac{W_U - W}{W} \times \frac{S}{S_U - S} \tag{5–6}$$

where S   = current stock price
      S_U = stock price at higher level
      W   = current warrant price
      W_U = warrant price resulting from stock price increase

If S_U equals 2 times S, then the equation simplifies as follows:

$$LR = \frac{\frac{W_U - W}{W}}{\frac{2S - S}{S}}$$

$$LR = \frac{W_U - W}{W} \tag{5–7}$$

Behavior of the leverage ratio is shown graphically in Exhibit 5–4. Figure 1 is the price curve for the warrant under consideration, and Figure 2 shows the curve for the leverage ratio. High values of the leverage ratio (≈ 2.5) are characteristic of undervalued warrants while low values of the leverage ratio (≈ 1.5) are indicative of undervalued warrants. The leverage ratio is not particularly sensitive to small stock price changes. The leverage ratio converges to 1.0 as the stock price advances well above the warrant exercise price.

Using data for the hypothetical warrant presented earlier (warrant price equals 6 when the stock price equals 20 and warrant price equals 20 1/2 if the stock price doubles to 40) the calculation for the leverage ratio is as follows:

$$LR = \frac{20.50 - 6}{6} = 2.4$$

THE MATHEMATICAL ADVANTAGE (MA)

The mathematical advantage is a tool designed to measure the relative merit of a warrant by comparing its leverage on the upside to its leverage on the downside. The tool was developed by Noddings [15] [2] and [16].

The mathematical advantage is defined as the ratio of the percentage increase in the warrant price given a 100 percent change in the warrant price compared to the percentage change in the warrant price given a 50 percent decline in the stock price. The two extremes, +100 percent and −50 percent, were chosen because they are equally likely to occur; that is, there is an equal probability that a stock will halve or double within any selected time interval. Expressed mathematically:

$$MA = \frac{\left.\frac{\Delta W}{\Delta S}\right|_{S = +100\%}}{\left.\frac{\Delta W}{\Delta S}\right|_{S = -50\%}}$$

$$MA = \left.\frac{\Delta W}{\Delta S}\right|_{S = +100\%} \times \left.\frac{\Delta S}{\Delta W}\right|_{S = -50\%} \qquad (5\text{–}8)$$

[2]Bracketed numbers refer to entries in the Bibliography, Appendix E.

EXHIBIT 5-4
The Leverage Ratio (LR)

FIGURE 1
WARRANT PRICE
CURVE

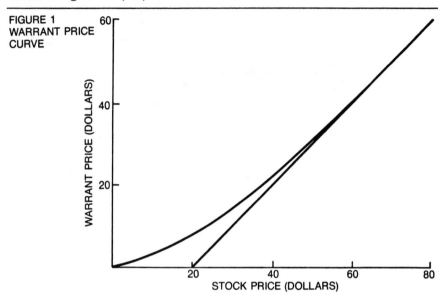

FIGURE 2
LEVERAGE RATIO

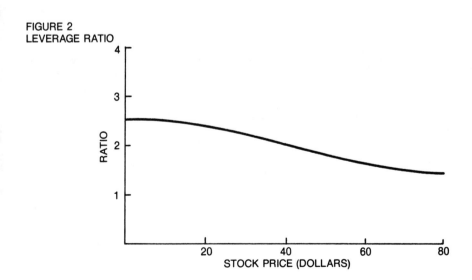

This expression can be rewritten in a form permitting rapid computation once the values of W are calculated at the stock price extremes:

$$MA = \frac{(.5)(W_U - W)}{W - W_D} \qquad (5\text{-}9)$$

where   MA = mathematical advantage
         S_U = stock price after 100% advance
         S_D = stock price after 50% decline
         W = prevailing warrant price
         W_U = warrant price after S increases 100%
         W_D = warrant price after S decreases 50%

Behavior of the mathematical advantage is shown diagrammatically in Exhibit 5–5. Figure 1 is the price curve for the warrant under consideration, and Figure 2 is a graph of the mathematical advantage.

Using data from the hypothetical example presented earlier in the chapter (the prevailing warrant price equals 6, W_U equals 20 1/2 and W_D equals 1 3/4) the calculation for the mathematical advantage is as follows:

$$MA = \frac{(.5)(20.50 - 6)}{(6 - 1.75)}$$

$$MA = 1.7$$

Compared with the minimum possible value of 1.00, this is an attractive number and verifies the earlier statement that the warrant is undervalued. Occasionally, even more attractive warrants can be found with levels of the mathematical advantage approaching 2.00.

THE MULTIPLE: STOCK OR WARRANT?

The various measures of merit—premium, the leverage indicator, the leverage ratio, and the mathematical advantage— are of most interest to traders or speculators anticipating a

EXHIBIT 5-5
Mathematical Advantage (MA)

FIGURE 1
WARRANT PRICE
CURVE

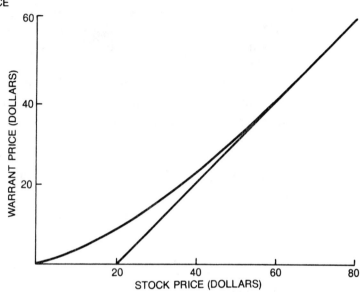

FIGURE 2
MATHEMATICAL
ADVANTAGE

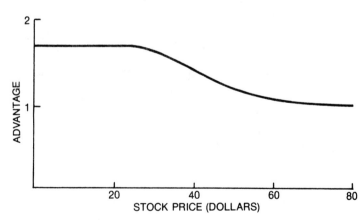

rapid advance in a stock's price which would be reflected immediately in the warrant. These indicators are not as useful to investors expecting a more casual price change.

A more meaningful piece of information to these investors is an indication as to which of the two, stock or warrant, is the better purchase over the long term; specifically, until warrant expiration. The *multiple* in two variations performs this function.

Determining which of the two, stock or warrant, is the better purchase is complicated by the fact that the warrant price includes a premium which decays as the warrant approaches expiration. This may, however, be balanced by the facts that (1) the warrant has leverage, and (2) for a given number of dollars more warrants can be purchased than common.

In the following paragraphs, two different multiples are examined. The first, M1, compares performance of equal dollar positions invested in the stock and warrant. It indicates the amount of appreciation necessary in the stock before the warrant position outperforms the stock position.

The second multiple, M2, compares changes in absolute value of the two securities. It indicates the amount of appreciation necessary in the stock to produce equivalent appreciation, on a percentage basis, in the warrant.

The behavior of M1 and M2 is shown graphically in Exhibit 5–6. Figure 1 is the price curve for the warrant under consideration. Figure 2 shows the variation of M1 for a broad range of stock prices, and Figure 3 is a graph of M2 over the same range of stock prices.

Appreciation Multiple (M1)

The multiple (M1) compares performance of equal dollar positions invested in the stock and warrant. It is annualized over the life of the warrant so that it indicates the percentage

EXHIBIT 5-6
Appreciation Multiples M1 and M2

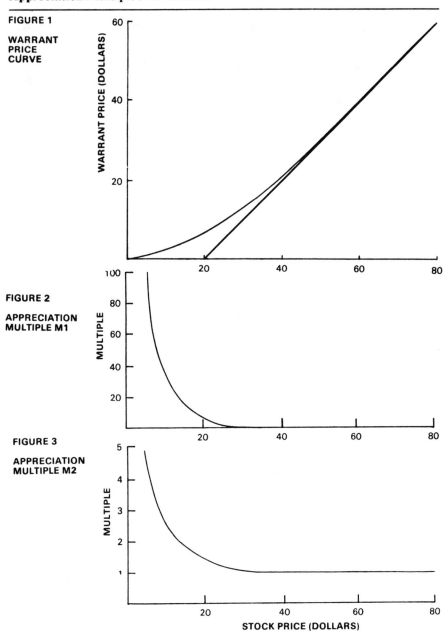

FIGURE 1

WARRANT PRICE CURVE

FIGURE 2

APPRECIATION MULTIPLE M1

FIGURE 3

APPRECIATION MULTIPLE M2

growth per year required in the stock for an equal investment in the warrant to have the same growth. This indicator was developed by Morrison [47].

If by the expiration date for the warrants the shares advance beyond a certain price (the breakeven price), the loss of the premium on the warrants will be more than offset by the fact that a given commitment can command a larger number of warrants than shares. Thus, while the absolute dollar appreciation on a warrant will be smaller than on a share, the larger number of warrants purchased may more than make up for this.

The first step in the calculation of the multiple M1 is the determination of the breakeven price. This is the price at which the common must sell at the expiration date of the warrants so that an equal capital appreciation will be achieved on the commitment of a given sum to either shares or warrants at current market prices.

Symbolically:

$$B = \frac{SE}{S - W}$$

where   B = breakeven price
         S = stock price
         E = exercise price
         W = warrant price

The necessary stock appreciation in dollars is:

$$G(\$) = B - S$$

where G($) = gain in dollars

The percentage increase is:

$$G(\%) = \frac{B - S}{S} \times 100$$

where G(%) = gain in percent

Finally, over the full life of the warrant, the percentage appreciation per year required of the common so that an equal investment in the warrants will match the growth of the same amount invested in stock:

$$\text{M1} = \frac{G(\%)}{t_e}$$

$$\text{M1} = \frac{E - (S - W)}{t_e(S - W)} \times 100$$

$$\text{M1} = \frac{E - S + W}{t_e(S - W)} \qquad\qquad (5\text{-}10)$$

where t_e = time until expiration

Using data from the hypothetical example presented earlier in the chapter (exercise price equals 20, stock price equals 20, warrant price equals 6, and time until expiration equals 4 years) the calculation of the appreciation multiple M1 is as follows:

$$\text{M1} = \frac{20 - 20 + 6}{(4)(20 - 6)} \times 100$$

$$\text{M1} = 10.7$$

Appreciation Multiple (M2)

Another approach to the same problem indentifies potential in a warrant by comparing the appreciation of a warrant from its current price to its price at expiration vis-à-vis the appreciation in the underlying common.

Assume that a warrant having premium and a finite life is purchased. If the underlying stock is unchanged at expiration, the warrants will reflect a loss in the amount of the premium. There is an increment by which the common must advance such that the increase in intrinsic value will offset the loss in the warrant premium. Under these circumstances the common would obviously have been a better purchase.

Additional appreciation in the common would cause appreciation in the warrant increasing on a percentage basis from less than that of the common to equal that of the common and finally to greater than that of the common. The stock price at which the appreciation of the warrant and common are equal is the transition point where the warrant becomes a better investment than the common.

A simple factor has been derived by Turov [71] which indicates the number of times the stock must appreciate for the warrant to have a value at expiration (i.e without a premium) representing the same amount of appreciation. Expressed algebraically:

$$M2 = \frac{E}{S - W} \qquad (5-11)$$

Using data from the hypothetical example presented earlier in the chapter (exercise price equals 20, stock price equals 20, warrant price equals 6, and time until expiration equals 4 years) the calculation of the appreciation multiple M2 is as follows:

$$M2 = \frac{20}{20 - 6}$$

$$M2 = 1.42$$

This means that if the stock has advanced by 42 percent (1.42 times the current price at the time the warrant expires), the warrant will have equally good performance. Note that this measure says nothing about the risk in owning the warrant or its performance on the downside as compared with the common. It merely indicates which of the two alternatives is preferable given that purchase of the stock for capital appreciation was contemplated.

PUTTING IT ALL TOGETHER

Only through practical experience is it possible to get a feel for the various indicators. Unfortunately, there is little consistency among them. High values indicate relative attractiveness for some while low values indicate relative attractiveness for others. Also, the range in values for different indicators determining the difference between highly desirable warrants and unattractive warrants may be large or small. Finally, the relationship between the stock price and the exercise price influences the magnitude of every indicator.

The intent of this section is to put all the indicators into perspective. A hypothetical stock and warrant are defined and the warrant assigned prices making it undervalued, fairly valued, and overvalued. The terms of these hypothetical securities are as follows:

exercise price = 20
conversion ratio = 1
expiration = 4 years
stock price = 20
stock volatility = 120 percent

With these terms, a fairly priced warrant could be expected to trade at about $8.00. For purposes of this example we will also look at the warrant statistics when it is trading at $6.00, approximately 25 percent undervalued, and when it is trading at $10.00, approximately 25 percent overvalued. The projected price curves for these warrants are shown in Exhibit 5-7. These curves are drawn according to a precise mathematical model which will be discussed in the following chapter. It is assumed that each warrant remains undervalued, fairly valued, or overpriced as the underlying stock price changes.

The value indicators for the undervalued warrant are shown in Exhibit 5-8. Calculations of the warrant evaluation tools for the fairly priced warrant are shown in Exhibit 5-9 (p. 58). Finally, calculations for the overpriced warrant are shown in Exhibit 5-10 (p. 59). As will be shown in subsequent chapters, the grossly undervalued or grossly overvalued warrants provide the most interesting investments. The indicators are useful to the extent they direct us to these situations.

EXHIBIT 5–7
**Price Curves for Three Hypothetical Warrants
Undervalued, Fairly Valued, and Overvalued**

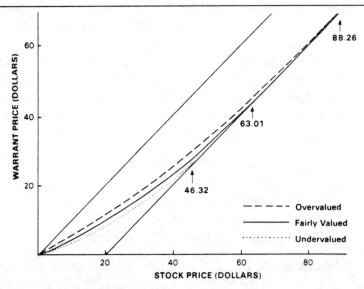

INDICATOR USEFULNESS

As mentioned earlier, each of the indicators provides useful information about the relative attractiveness of a warrant. However, none of the indicators discussed so far incorporates all of the factors which influence a warrant's price. Therefore, considerable experience is required in using the simple indicators, and personal judgment must always be incorporated in the investment decision.

The following paragraphs discuss each of the indicators in more specific detail. Included is the range in the value of the indicator for a range of stock prices or, more specifically, for a range in the normalized stock price (S/E). Three types of warrants are examined: those which are undervalued, those which are fairly valued, and those which are overvalued. The attributes and shortcomings of the indicators are addressed as well as special pitfalls.

EXHIBIT 5–8
Value Indicators for an Undervalued Warrant

Stock Price Exchange	– 75%	– 50%	– 25%	0%	+ 25%	+ 50%	+ 100%	+ 300%
Stock Price	5	10	15	20	25	30	40	80
Warrant Price	0.52	1.77	3.62	6.00	8.89	12.25	20.33	60.00
Warrant Price Change	– 91%	– 71%	– 40%	0%	+ 48%	+ 104%	+ 238%	+ 900%
Warrant Intrinsic Value	0	0	0	0	5	10	20	60
Normalized Stock Price (S/E)	.25	.50	.75	1.00	1.25	1.50	2.00	4.00
Normalized Warrant Price (W/E)	.03	.09	.18	.30	.44	.61	1.02	3.00
Premium (P1)	10.4	17.7	24.1	30.0	15.6	7.5	0.8	0.0
Premium (P2)	310.4	117.7	57.5	30.0	15.6	7.5	0.8	0.0
Leverage Indicator (LI)	9.6	5.6	4.1	3.3	2.8	2.4	2.0	1.3
Leverage Ratio (LR)	2.4	2.4	2.4	2.4	2.4	2.3	2.0	1.3
Mathematical Advantage (MA)	1.7	1.7	1.7	1.7	1.7	1.6	1.4	1.0
Appreciation Multiple (M1)	86.6	35.8	18.9	10.7	6.0	3.2	0.4	0.0
Appreciation Multiple (M2)	4.5	2.4	1.8	1.4	1.2	1.1	1.0	1.0

Premium (P1)

The behavior of the premium (P1) is shown in Exhibit 5–11
for undervalued, fairly valued, and overvalued warrants
given a wide range in the factor S/E. The indicator has a
fin-shaped curve increasing from zero when S/E equals zero
and gradually increasing to a peak value when S/E equals
one. For long term warrants the peak value may be under 30 if
the warrant is grossly undervalued. For overpriced warrants
the peak value may be 50 or higher. As S/E increases further,
the indicator decreases gradually reaching zero once again
when S/E reaches a value of 3 or 4. Of course the level of the
premium is meaningless if S/E is not known.

EXHIBIT 5-9
Value Indicators for a Fairly Valued Warrant

Stock Price Change	- 75%	- 50%	- 25%	0%	+ 25%	+ 50%	+ 100%	+ 300%
Stock Price	5	10	15	20	25	30	40	80
Warrant Price	1.05	2.90	5.25	8.00	11.10	14.50	22.10	60.00
Warrant Price Change	- 87%	- 64%	- 34%	0%	+ 26%	+ 81%	+ 176%	+ 650%
Warrant Intrinsic Value	0	0	0	0	5	10	20	60
Normalized Stock Price (S/E)	.25	.50	.75	1.00	1.25	1.50	2.00	4.00
Normalized Warrant Price (W/E)	.05	.15	.26	.40	.56	.73	1.11	3.00
Premium (P1)	21.0	29.0	35.0	40.0	24.4	15.0	5.30	0.0
Premium (P2)	321.0	129.0	68.3	40.0	24.4	15.0	5.3	0.0
Leverage Indicator (LI)	4.8	3.4	2.9	2.5	2.3	2.1	1.8	1.3
Leverage Ratio (LR)	1.8	1.8	1.8	1.8	1.8	1.8	1.7	1.3
Mathematical Advantage (MA)	1.4	1.4	1.4	1.4	1.4	1.4	1.3	1.0
Appreciation Multiple (M1)	101.6	45.4	26.3	16.7	11.0	7.3	2.9	0.0
Appreciation Multiple (M2)	5.1	2.8	2.1	1.7	1.4	1.3	1.1	1.0

Premium (P2)

The behavior of the premium (P2) is shown in Exhibit 5-12 for undervalued, fairly valued, and overvalued warrants given a wide range in the factor S/E. When S/E is low, P2 is high, sometimes reaching levels exceeding 1,000. The indicator gradually declines to zero as S/E reaches a value of 3 or 4. In fact, the calculations for P1 and P2 are identical for all values of S/E greater than or equal to one. For the examples shown, the magnitude of P2 is similar regardless of the warrant relative valuation. Because of this poor resolution, the usefulness of this indicator is limited. P1 is a superior measure of premium and is the indicator with which analysts should become most familiar.

EXHIBIT 5–10
Value Indicators for an Overvalued Warrant

	−75%	−50%	−25%	0%	+25%	+50%	+100%	+300%
Stock Price Change	−75%	−50%	−25%	0%	+25%	+50%	+100%	+300%
Stock Price	5	10	15	20	25	30	40	80
Warrant Price	1.67	4.09	6.90	10.00	13.36	16.91	24.53	60.12
Warrant Price Change	−83%	−59%	−31%	0%	+34%	+69%	+145%	+501%
Warrant Intrinsic Value	0	0	0	0	5	10	20	60
Normalized Stock Price (S/E)	.25	.50	.75	1.00	1.25	1.50	2.00	4.00
Normalized Warrant Price (W/E)	.08	.20	.35	.50	.67	.85	1.23	3.01
Premium (P1)	33.4	40.9	46.0	50.0	33.4	23.0	11.3	0.2
Premium (P2)	333.4	140.9	79.3	50.0	33.4	23.0	11.3	0.2
Leverage Indicator (LI)	3.0	2.4	2.2	2.0	1.9	1.8	1.6	1.3
Leverage Ratio (LR)	1.5	1.5	1.5	1.5	1.5	1.5	1.5	1.3
Mathematical Advantage (MA)	1.2	1.2	1.2	1.2	1.2	1.2	1.2	1.1
Appreciation Multiple (M1)	125.2	59.6	36.7	25.0	18.0	13.2	7.3	0.2
Appreciation Multiple (M2)	6.0	3.4	2.5	2.0	1.7	1.5	1.3	1.0

Leverage Indicator (LI)

The behavior of the leverage indicator is shown in Exhibit 5–13 for undervalued, fairly valued, and overvalued warrants given a wide range in the factor S/E. The indicator is

EXHIBIT 5–11
The Warrant Premium (P1)
Behavior as a Function of Warrant Valuation and
Position in the Warrant Diagram

Normalized Stock Price (S/E)	.25	.50	.75	1.00	1.25	1.50	2.00	4.00
Undervalued Warrant	10.4	17.7	24.1	30.0	15.6	7.5	0.8	0.0
Fairly Valued Warrant	21.0	29.0	35.0	40.0	24.4	15.0	5.3	0.0
Overvalued Warrant	33.4	40.9	46.0	50.0	33.4	23.0	11.3	0.2

EXHIBIT 5-12
The Warrant Premium (P2)
Behavior as a Function of Warrant Valuation and
Position in the Warrant Diagram

Normalized Stock Price (S/E)	.25	.50	.75	1.00	1.25	1.50	2.00	4.00
Undervalued Warrant	310.4	117.7	57.5	30.0	15.6	7.5	0.8	0.0
Fairly Valued Warrant	321.4	129.0	68.3	40.0	24.4	15.0	5.3	0.0
Overvalued Warrant	333.4	140.9	79.3	50.0	33.4	23.0	11.3	0.2

high (values in excess of 10 for undervalued warrants) when S/E is low and gradually decreases to a value of one as S/E increases. When S/E is below one the resolution of this indicator between warrants of different valuations is excellent. When valuing long-term warrants this is an excellent tool to turn to first.

Leverage Ratio (LR)

The behavior of the leverage ratio is shown in Exhibit 5–14 for undervalued, fairly valued, and overvalued warrants given a wide range in the factor S/E. The indicator is high (values in excess of 3 for undervalued warrants) when S/E is low and

EXHIBIT 5-13
The Leverage Indicator (LI)
Behavior as a Function of Warrant
Valuation and Position in the Warrant Diagram

Normalized Stock Price (S/E)	.25	.50	.75	1.00	1.25	1.50	2.00	4.00
Undervalued Warrant	9.6	5.6	4.1	3.3	2.8	2.4	2.0	1.3
Fairly Valued Warrant	4.8	3.4	2.9	2.5	2.3	2.1	1.8	1.3
Overvalued Warrant	3.0	2.4	2.2	2.0	1.9	1.8	1.6	1.3

EXHIBIT 5-14
The Leverage Ratio (LR)
Behavior as a Function of Warrant
Valuation and Position in the Warrant Diagram

Normalized Stock Price (S/E)	.25	.50	.75	1.00	1.25	1.50	2.00	4.00
Undervalued Warrant	2.4	2.4	2.4	2.4	2.4	2.3	2.0	1.3
Fairly Valued Warrant	1.8	1.8	1.8	1.8	1.8	1.8	1.7	1.3
Overvalued Warrant	1.5	1.5	1.5	1.5	1.5	1.5	1.5	1.3

gradually decreases to a value of 1 as S/E increases. Although the leverage ratio is generally discussed in books and manuals on warrant investing, its usefulness must be questioned since the value of the indicator is relatively constant for large ranges in the value of S/E. In addition, because of its low value, the absolute difference between values of the indicator for undervalued warrants and overvalued warrants is small. This masks the fact that the percentage difference between the two is large.

Mathematical Advantage (MA)

The behavior of the mathematical advantage is shown in Exhibit 5-15 for undervalued, fairly valued, and overvalued warrants given a wide range in the factor S/E. The value ranges between 1 and 2, for undervalued and overvalued warrants and, as is the case with the leverage ratio, the value of the indicator is relatively constant for large excursions in the value of S/E. The percentage difference between attractive levels of the indicator and unattractive levels is significant even though the absolute difference is small. Thus the indicator is of value in discriminating between warrants and is worthy of consideration when making an investment decision.

EXHIBIT 5-15
The Mathematical Advantage (MA)
Behavior as a Function of Warrant
Valuation and Position in the Warrant Diagram

Normalized Stock Price (S/E)	.25	.50	.75	1.00	1.25	1.50	2.00	4.00
Undervalued Warrant	1.7	1.7	1.7	1.7	1.7	1.6	1.4	1.0
Fairly Valued Warrant	1.4	1.4	1.4	1.4	1.4	1.4	1.3	1.0
Overvalued Warrant	1.2	1.2	1.2	1.2	1.2	1.2	1.2	1.1

Appreciation Multiple (M1)

The behavior of the appreciation multiple (M1) is shown in
Exhibit 5-16 for undervalued, fairly valued, and overvalued
warrants given a wide range in the factor S/E. The calculations assume a warrant life of four years. The indicator has
values in the vicinity of one hundred when S/E is low and
gradually decreases to zero as S/E increases. For the levels of
S/E which are generally of interest, this indicator exhibits
large percentage differences between warrants which are
undervalued and warrants which are overvalued. M1 serves
well its function in helping to determine which is the better
buy—stock or warrant.

EXHIBIT 5-16
The Appreciation Multiple (M1)
Behavior as a Function of Warrant
Valuation and Position in the Warrant Diagram

Normalized Stock Price (S/E)	.25	.50	.75	1.00	1.25	1.50	2.00	4.00
Undervalued Warrant	86.6	35.8	18.9	10.7	6.0	3.2	0.4	0.0
Fairly Valued Warrant	101.6	45.4	26.3	16.7	11.0	9.2	2.9	0.0
Overvalued Warrant	125.2	59.6	36.7	25.0	18.0	13.2	7.3	0.2

EXHIBIT 5-17
The Appreciation Multiple (M2)
Behavior as a Function of Warrant
Valuation and Position in the Warrant Diagram

Normalized Stock Price (S/E)	.25	.50	.75	1.00	1.25	1.50	2.00	4.00
Undervalued Warrant	4.5	2.4	1.8	1.4	1.2	1.1	1.0	1.0
Fairly Valued Warrant	5.1	2.8	2.1	1.7	1.4	1.3	1.1	1.0
Overvalued Warrant	6.0	3.4	2.5	2.0	1.7	1.5	1.3	1.0

Appreciation Multiple (M2)

The behavior of the appreciation multiple (M2) is shown in Exhibit 5-17 for undervalued, fairly valued, and overvalued warrants given a wide range in the factor S/E. The indicator has values in the vicinity of 5 for low values of S/E and gradually decreases to 1 as S/E increases. The indicator clearly delineates the advantage of undervalued warrants with respect to overvalued warrants and also assists greatly in the stock or warrant purchase decision.

CHAPTER
6

ADVANCED ANALYTICAL TECHNIQUES

INTRODUCTION

Conceptually a mathematical warrant pricing model is very appealing. In its ultimate form it would incorporate every factor which impacts a warrant's price. A few numbers would be entered on a computer keyboard and almost instantly the true theoretical value of the warrant would be determined. Devising an investment strategy would be simple and straightforward. The computed value would be compared with the value assigned to the warrant in the marketplace. Overvalued issues would be incorporated in strategies involving warrant sales and short sales. Undervalued issues would be incorporated in strategies involving warrant purchases.

Unfortunately such a model is not available now and it is unlikely that it ever will be. The derivation of such a model is a complex undertaking and represents a project working at the state of the art in investment theory. This does not imply that meaningful work in this area is unavailable—just that the final solution has not yet been attained.

Unfortunate also is the fact that existing work on the subject is extremely theoretical. It is both profound and complex. It is a challenge for professionals to incorporate such work into their efforts, and it is nearly impossible for the average investor to decipher.

Nevertheless, a rigorous approach is needed to estimate a warrant's fair value, and simplified theory can be tapped to supply this framework, even if the result is not correct to three decimal places. As will be shown subsequently, the research can be reduced to a simple and straightforward methodology which enables rapid and accurate estimation of the price at which a warrant should trade.

WARRANT MODELS

Broadly speaking, warrant models can be classified into two general categories. These can be defined as empirical models which describe how warrants *do* trade and theoretical models which describe how warrants *should* trade.

Empirical Models

Models describing how warrants *do* trade are determined by examination of historical and current statistics. Warrants having similar characteristics are examined as a group, and the average or typical price is determined. The techniques for performing this type of research are generally complex and involve mathematical processes such as regression analysis.

An outstanding description of the required methodology is provided in Kassouf [11].

Theoretical Models

Models describing how warrants *should* trade are derived directly from the theory of finance, in particular option theory. Historical prices are not a factor in defining these models. Pioneering work in this area was conducted by Sprenkle [63] (1961), Samuelson [56] (1965), McKean [44] (1965), Van Horne [74] (1969), and Samuelson and Merton [57] (1969). Later work focused not so much on warrants in particular but on options in general. The contribution by Black and Scholes [30] (1973) provided researchers with fresh insight, the impact of which is still being measured.

As to which approach is best is a subject of controversy unlikely to be resolved by pure logic. Warrant premiums have a life of their own influenced not only by factors which can be defined precisely and measured but also by less tangible factors such as sentiment. A few of the factors which have been examined with inconclusive results are listed below:

1. Exchange listing. Early investigators found a correlation between a warrant's price and its listing status. Shelton [61] found that listed warrants (at that time warrants traded only on the American Stock Exchange) were more valuable than those trading over-the-counter.

2. Competing products. The availability of similar securities—in particular, listed options—influences the price of a warrant. Excellent opportunities for selling warrants short have appeared just prior to the introduction of call options on the same underlying stock.

3. Price history of the common. It is not only the historical volatility of the common but also its recent price behavior that influences the warrant's premium.

The rigorous approaches do not take into account factors such as market sentiment, emotion, or prevailing premium levels. Thus, although a theoretical model will identify a mispriced warrant, profits from the situation may not materialize quickly and may never appear. Some warrants remain relatively cheap or dear for extended periods although rationality usually prevails in the long run. Nevertheless, a theoretical model highlights the warrants which may be of interest and gives the investor a convenient way of screening the numerous candidates.

SURVEY OF HISTORICAL RESEARCH

The purpose of this chapter is not to explore all the techniques developed for warrant analysis. It is intended to give the reader the flavor of the various approaches and to converge on a methodology which is accurate and easy to use. Researchers wishing to explore the models presented here in further depth or to locate other models are referred to Appendix E. The extensive bibliography contains a comprehensive listing of books, articles, and private publications devoted to the subject.

Although warrants have existed for more than 75 years, there is little documentation regarding these issues in the literature prior to 1950, and serious material did not appear until the mid 1960s. The last complete book addressing the matter was that of Prendergast [18] published in 1973.

Giguère Model (1958)

One of the earliest attempts at quantifying warrant-stock price relationships was published in the late 50s by Guynemer Giguère [34]. Although elementary by current standards, his analysis clearly defined the problem as it was then understood and resulted in a model which described reality. The formula which Giguère developed is shown in Exhibit 6-1.

EXHIBIT 6-1
Giguère Warrant Model

$$W = \frac{S^2}{4E}\bigg|_{S \leq 2E} \qquad (6-1)$$

$$W = S - E\big|_{W > 2E} \qquad (6-2)$$

$$\omega = nW \qquad (6-3)$$

where S = stock price
     E = exercise price
    W = warrant price per share
     n = conversion ratio
    ω = traded warrant price

Giguère correctly identified some of the basic determinants of warrant pricing—namely, longevity and the relationship of the stock price to the exercise price. However, in his work there is no consideration of stock volatility, stock yield, potential dilution, or prevailing interest rates.

The graph described by equations (6-1) and (6-2) is a parabola which conforms to real world observations. The values it produces lie on a curve which approaches zero smoothly as the stock price approaches zero. It also meets the intrinsic value line tangentially when the stock price is twice the exercise price.

In order to compare the various warrant models, a solution for each is provided in the accompanying text. The example used is the Sperry Rand warrant which was issued in the early 1960s and expired in 1966. This warrant was selected because data are available for the stock and the warrant which are necessary for solving all of the models. In particular, it existed during the period when the Kassouf model (to be discussed subsequently) was developed, and this model cannot be used with confidence in different time periods.

Statistics for the Sperry Rand securities are given in Exhibit 6–2. The solution of the Giguère model for the Sperry Rand warrant is given in Exhibit 6–3. Of course time is not a factor in Giguère's equation, but he did recognize its influence and he would have lowered the warrant's projected price to account for its short life.

Samuelson Model (1965)

Relatively unsophisticated analysis predominated until 1965. That this was the case should not be surprising since the discipline was relatively unexplored and complex. However, the warrant did not escape the attention of the academics who applied rigorous mathematics in the attempt to characterize this fascinating security.

Among the first was Paul A. Samuelson [56], the noted economist, working at the time at the Massachusetts Institute of Technology. In conjunction with Henry McKean, Jr. [56], also of M.I.T., they developed a model for evaluating perpetual warrants but claims as to the effectiveness for warrants

---

EXHIBIT 6–2
Security Statistics
Sperry Rand Corporation
Industry Group: Computers and Peripherals
November 1966

Common Stock		Warrant	
Price	27	Price	8.125
Volatility	.54*	Exercise Price	25.926
Dividend	0	Expiration	9-15-67
52-Week High	$33\frac{5}{8}$	Issue Size	3,847,834
52-Week Low	$17\frac{1}{8}$	Conversion Ratio	1.08
S&P Rank	B	Time Remaining	.833 years
Shares Outstanding	30,805,724	52-Week High	$13\frac{1}{4}$
		52-Week Low	6

*Annualized standard deviation

EXHIBIT 6–3
Giguère Warrant Model
Sample Solution

Issue:	Sperry Rand Warrants
Evalution Date:	November 15, 1966
Warrant Price:	8.125
Equation Variables:	$S = 27$
	$E = 25.926$

Solution:
$$W = \frac{S^2}{4E} = \frac{(27)^2}{(4)(25.926)}$$
$$W = 7.03$$
$$\omega = nW = (1.08)(7.03)$$
$$\omega = 7.59$$

Answer:
$$W = 7.03$$
$$\omega = 7.59$$

EXHIBIT 6–4
Samuelson Warrant Model

$$W = E(c - 1)\left(\frac{S}{Ec}\right)^{c/c - 1} \tag{6-4}$$

$$c = \frac{\left(\frac{1}{2} - \frac{\alpha}{\sigma^2}\right) + \sqrt{\left[\frac{1}{2} + \frac{\alpha}{\sigma^2}\right]^2 + 2\left[\frac{\beta - \alpha}{\sigma^2}\right]}}{\left(\frac{1}{2} + \frac{\alpha}{\sigma^2}\right) + \sqrt{\left[\frac{1}{2} + \frac{\alpha}{\sigma^2}\right]^2 + 2\left[\frac{\beta - \alpha}{\sigma^2}\right]} - 1} \tag{6-5}$$

$$\omega = nW \tag{6-6}$$

where S = stock price
E = exercise price
W = warrant price per share
n = conversion ratio
w = traded warrant price
α = projected growth rate of the common stock
β = warrant's required growth rate
σ = stock's average departure from the trend line

having expiration dates were never made. The derivation of the model is highly mathematical and even in a simplified version as shown in Exhibit 6–4 it is complex. Nevertheless, this model is valuable and, as will be shown subsequently, with a little massaging it will play an important part in the development of an evaluation approach suitable for many investors in selecting warrant issues for their portfolios.

To use this model the investor must make several forecasts. These include the average growth rate of the stock, and the volatility of the stock; that is, about how far on average the actual prices will deviate from the expected growth trend line. The investor must also supply a judgment about how much faster than the stock the warrant must grow in order to justify its purchase.

The formal Samuelson model applies only to perpetual warrants (warrants which have no expiration such as those for Atlas Corp.). Samuelson himself did not develop a formula covering the general case of finite warrants and expressed doubt that a neat and tidy formula (known mathematically as a closed-form solution) would ever surface. In other words, mathematicians and practitioners would always have to be content with numerical approximations. However, the model can be adapted for use with more than just perpetual warrants.

The Samuelson model using McKean's [56] solution is restated in Exhibit 6–5 where gamma is the parameter that differs across warrants of different characteristics. This model has several attributes. The curve which it generates converges on the appropriate boundaries for high and low values of the optioned common stock. Also, the values which it produces conform well to observed prices. Finally, the model is easily entered into a programmable calculator or personal computer permitting rapid evaluations of warrant premiums and price projections.

Kassouf Model (1965)

Sheen T. Kassouf [10], [11], [24], [39], and [40] was also an early researcher into warrant pricing. His work was rigorous

---

EXHIBIT 6-5
Samuelson-McKean Model Restated

$$W = (E)(c - 1)\left(\frac{S}{cE}\right)^{\gamma} \Bigg|_{S \leq cE} \qquad (6\text{-}7)$$

$$W = S - E \Bigg|_{S > cE} \qquad (6\text{-}8)$$

$$c = \frac{\gamma}{\gamma - 1} \qquad (6\text{-}9)$$

$$\omega = nW \qquad (6\text{-}10)$$

where S = stock price
      E = exercise price
      γ = a parameter that differs across warrants of
           different characteristics
      W = warrant price per share
      n = conversion ratio
      ω = traded warrant price

---

and used advanced mathematical techniques. His research was mostly empirical and focused on fitting curves to a vast data base of warrant statistics which he had collected. The model which he developed is summarized in Exhibit 6-6.

The central element of Kassouf's work is the simple hyperbola shown in equation (6-11). The value of "z" (which can vary between 1 and infinity) determines the height and curvature of the warrant price track. This model conforms to the boundary conditions of the warrant diagram and the price curves it produces fit empirical data with great accuracy.

Kassouf postulated the factors which influence a warrant's price and, based on an analysis of data covering a period of 20 years, quantified the impact of these factors on the price of the warrant. In its final iteration the model incorporates the stock price, the exercise price, the conversion ratio, the stock dividend, the potential dilution caused by warrant exercise (number of outstanding warrants/number of outstanding common shares), and recent stock price history (mean of previous 11 month high and low).

EXHIBIT 6–6
Kassouf Warrant Model

$$W = E\left\{\left[\left(\frac{S}{E}\right)^z + 1\right]^{1/z} - 1\right\} \qquad (6\text{--}11)$$

$$z = 1.307 + \frac{5.355}{T} + 14.257\,R + .298\,D + 1.015\ln\left(\frac{S}{X}\right) + .405\left(\frac{S}{E}\right) \qquad (6\text{--}12)$$

$$\omega = nW \qquad (6\text{--}13)$$

where S = stock price
    E = exercise price per share
    W = warrant price per share
    T = months remaining before expiration
    R = annual stock dividend per share
    $D = \dfrac{\text{number of new shares if all options are exercised}}{\text{number of outstanding common shares}}$
    $\overline{X}$ = mean of previous eleven months high-low average
    ln = natural logarithm
    n = conversion ratio
    ω = traded warrant price

Using a technique known as multiple regression, the numerical value for each input was determined and incorporated into the "z" factor. The formula for "z" in its final form is shown in equation 6–12.

The Kassouf model has the following features. It determines a warrant's price based on the price of other warrants which were in the sample used to determine the various numerical coefficients in "z." It does not provide a theoretical value based on principles of finance or option theory. If all warrants in the test sample were relatively cheap or dear, a warrant being evaluated by the model would be assigned a value which was also cheap or dear by comparison.

In addition, the coefficients vary over time in response to secular changes in the warrant market. Therefore equation (6–12) is no longer valid since the data used in its derivation are nearly 20 years old. To be useful today, a complete mathematical analysis of recent historical price data would be necessary to update the coefficients.

The equations for the Kassouf model are easily entered into a programmable pocket calculator. A sample solution is provided in Exhibit 6–7 for the Sperry Rand warrant. Using the model, the projected price for the Sperry Rand warrant was 9.97 as compared with the actual price of 8.13.

When z = 2, Equation 6–11 simplifies to:

$$W = \sqrt{E^2 + S'} - E \qquad (6\text{–}14)$$

EXHIBIT 6–7
Kassouf Warrant Model
Sample Solution

Issue	Sperry Rand Warrants
Evaluation Date	November 15, 1966
Warrant Price	8.125
Equation Variables	S = 27
	n = 1.08
	E = 25.926
	T = 10 (months)
	R = 0 (dividend in dollars)
	D = .12
	$\overline{X}$ = 23.49

Solution

$$z = 1.307 + \frac{5.355}{10} + (.298)(.12) + (1.015)\ln\left(\frac{27}{23.49}\right) + (.405)\left(\frac{27}{25.926}\right)$$

$$= 1.307 + .5355 + .036 + .141 + .422$$

$$z = 2.441$$

$$W = 25.926\left\{\left[\left(\frac{27}{25.926}\right)^{2.44} + 1\right]^{1/2.44} - 1\right\}$$

$$= (25.926)[(1.104 + 1)^{.410} - 1]$$

$$= (25.926)(.356)$$

$$W = 9.241$$

$$\omega = (1.08)(9241)$$

$$\omega = 9.98$$

Answer: z = 2.44
           ω = 9.98

This model does a good job of approximating the price of long term warrants on volatile, non-dividend paying stocks, and it is frequently used as a starting point for evaluating warrants having different characteristics.

Shelton Model (1967)

John Shelton conducted his research on warrants in the early 60s, and his results were published in 1967 [61]. His work was empirical. He correctly identified many of the factors influencing warrant prices and experimented with curves which fit observed data. Shelton was aware of the Samuelson study [56], but it did not influence his own work. Similarly, he was aware of the early investigations of Kassouf [68] but not of the more advanced work which Kassouf completed subsequently [69].

Shelton identified the following factors as important in determining the price of a warrant:

1. The relationship of the stock price to the exercise price,
2. The common stock yield,
3. Whether or not the warrant was listed, and
4. The longevity of the warrant.

Shelton's analysis began by redefining the zone of plausible prices where a warrant could trade in the warrant diagram. In particular, Shelton derived an upper limit considerably tighter than the straight line characterized by the equation $S = W$ shown in Exhibit 1–2. Shelton used as the upper limit of a warrant's price the locus of points for which percentage changes are equal for both stock and warrant holders. This refined boundary condition is shown in Exhibit 6–8.

Shelton also observed that warrants seldom sell above their intrinsic value when the stock is trading at four or more times the exercise price. At that point the investor becomes indifferent to ownership of the stock or warrant (assuming a

EXHIBIT 6–8
Shelton Warrant Model
Zone of Plausible Prices

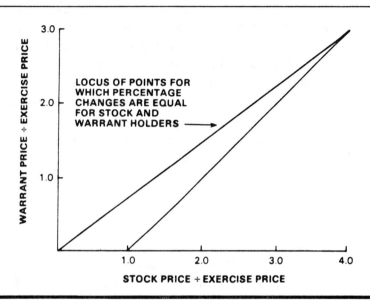

EXHIBIT 6–9
Shelton Warrant Model

$$W = (W_{max} - W_{min}) \left[\sqrt[4]{\frac{t}{72}} \left(.47 - 4.25\frac{D}{S} + .17L \right) \right] + W_{min} \qquad (6\text{–}15)$$

$$W_{max} = .75S \qquad (6\text{–}16)$$

$$W_{min} = S - E \qquad (6\text{–}17)$$

$$\omega = nW \qquad (6\text{–}18)$$

where S = stock price
   E = exercise price per share
   W = warrant price per share
   D = stock dividend in dollars
   t = warrant duration in months
   L = 0 if warrant trading over the counter; 1 if warrant listed
   n = conversion ratio
   ω = traded warrant price

dividendless stock) because the percentage gain or loss in holding the warrant would be the same as the percentage gain or loss in holding the stock.

The Shelton warrant model is given in Exhibit 6–9. Although expressed in somewhat awkward terms, Equation 6–15 accomplishes the following. It establishes the price zone allowable for a warrant given the stock price; it calculates the percentage of that price zone appropriate for the warrant; and it adds the permissible value to the warrant intrinsic value to determine the net warrant price. It also includes a factor which accounts for the decay in warrant premium with time as observed in the marketplace:

$$\sqrt[4]{t/72}$$

The remaining factors account for the negative bias introduced if the stock has yield and for positive bias if the warrant is listed.

A solution for the Sperry Rand warrants using the Shelton model is given in Exhibit 6–10. Using the model, the projected price for the Sperry Rand warrant was 9.98 as compared with the actual price of 8.13.

Shelton found no dependence of a warrant's price on the volatility or price history of the underlying stock. However, it must be remembered that he was an early researcher pioneering this type of analysis, and the sample of warrants used in his work was small (less than 40). This factor makes the Shelton model of questionable value today even though it is interesting historically.

Black-Scholes Model (1973)

The Black-Scholes model is a theoretical model derived from principles of finance in an attempt to determine how options should be priced. The model was introduced at about the same time the Chicago Board Options Exchange opened for business, and its use in evaluating listed options gave the

---

EXHIBIT 6–10
Shelton Warrant Model
Sample Solution

Example:	Sperry Rand Warrants
Date:	November 15, 1966
Warrant Price:	8.125
Equation Variables:	$S = 27$
	$D = 0$
	$t = 10$
	$L = 1$
	$n = 1.08$

Solution:

$$W = (W_{max} - W_{min})\left[\sqrt[4]{\frac{t}{72}}(.47 - 4.25\frac{D}{S} + .17L)\right] + W_{min}$$

$$W_{max} = .75S = (.75)(27) = 20.25$$

$$W_{min} = S - E = 27 - 25.926 = 1.074$$

$$W = (20.25 - 1.074)\left[\sqrt[4]{\frac{10}{72}}(.47 + .17)\right] + 1.074$$

$$= (19.176)[(.61)(.64)] + 1.074$$

$$W = 8.56$$

$$\omega = (1.08)(8.56)$$

Answer: $\omega = 9.25$

---

model immediate and widespread popularity. Although used primarily for evaluating puts and calls, it is applicable to any option-like instrument including warrants.

The model is described fully in Exhibit 6–11. As can be seen from Equation 6–19, the model is rather complex and comments regarding its derivation and the meaning of the various terms are beyond the scope of this text. In order to use the Black-Scholes Equation 6–20. The dilution factor "q" is defined as the ratio of the number of warrants issued to the number of shares of common stock outstanding. A sample solution using the Black-Scholes model for the Sperry Rand warrant is shown in Exhibit 6–12.

EXHIBIT 6-11
Black-Scholes Model

$$W' = SN(d_1) - EN(d_2)e^{-rt} \qquad (6\text{-}19)$$

$$d_1 = \frac{\ln(\frac{S}{E}) + (r + \frac{1}{2}\sigma^2)t}{\sigma\sqrt{t}}$$

$$d_2 = d_1 - \sigma\sqrt{t}$$

$$W = \frac{W'}{1+q} \qquad (6\text{-}20)$$

$$q = \frac{\text{number of warrants issued}}{\text{number of common shares outstanding}} \qquad (6\text{-}21)$$

$$\omega = nW$$

where   S = stock price
        E = exercise price
        W' = warrant price per share before dilution adjustment
        W = warrant price per share after dilution adjustment
        N(d) = cumulative normal density function
        T = time until expiration
        e = 2.7182818
        r = risk free interest rate
        σ = standard deviation of stock returns
        n = conversion ratio
        ω = traded warrant price

The adjustment for dilution is this example is not entirely accurate. To be precise the Black-Scholes model requires that the value of the warrant be computed for the firm without warrants already outstanding. In addition, certain of the variables used in the equation—namely, the stock price and variance—must be the values that would prevail in the absence of outstanding warrants. Thus, the solution calculated in Exhibit 6-11 should be studied to learn how the problem should be approached rather than as an exact means of determining the price for this particular warrant. Later in this

---

EXHIBIT 6–12
Black-Scholes Model—Sample Solution

Issue:	Sperry Rand Warrants
Evalution date:	November 15, 1966
Warrant price:	8.125
Equation variables:	$S = 27$
	$E = 25.926$
	$t = .833$ years
	$r = .0525$
	$\sigma = .536$

Solution:

$$d_1 = \frac{\ln\left(\frac{27}{25.926}\right) + \left[.0525 + \frac{(.536)^2}{2}\right](.833)}{.536\sqrt{.833}}$$

$$= \frac{.041 + (.0525 + .144)(.833)}{(.536)(.913)}$$

$$= \frac{.205}{.489}$$

$$d_1 = .417$$

$$d_2 = .417 - (.536)(\sqrt{.833})$$

$$d_2 = -.0722$$

$$N(d_1) = .662*$$

$$N(d_2) = .071*$$

$$W' = SN(d_1) - EN(d_2)e^{-rt}$$

$$= (27)(.662) - (25.926)(.471)e^{-(.0525)(.833)}$$

$$W' = 6.19$$

$$q = \frac{3,847,834}{30,805,724}$$

$$q = .125$$

$$W = \frac{6.19}{1 + .125}$$

$$W = 5.50$$

$$\omega = (1.08)(5.50)$$

Answer: $\omega = 5.94$

---

*Methods for determining N(d) are provided in Appendix C.

chapter, the Black-Scholes model is used in the proper manner to determine the price at which warrants would trade, should they be issued.

The Black-Scholes model is also easily entered into a programmable calculator or personal computer. The factor N(d) —the area under the normal curve and to the left of x—is not readily calculated. A simple method for approximating this factor is given in Appendix C.

Value Line Model

Value Line, the investment advisory service, publishes *Options & Convertibles* (see Appendix A), a periodical which provides regular coverage of all actively traded warrants. The analysis is extensive and thorough and includes an estimation of fair value as well as other information and statistics which are quite valuable.

The Value Line approach to determining fair value (or, using their terminology, normal value) relies on empirical rather than theoretical projections. The current warrant price is viewed in relationship to its historical price under like conditions. If the issue was not traded, similar issues are examined.

Value Line then assigns a price curve (track) to the warrant projecting prices at which it would trade if it were normally valued. The deviation between the estimated price and the traded price is the amount by which the option is overvalued or undervalued. Value Line has observed that there is a tendency for warrants to remain off the projected track. Hence, they do not project that the warrant will return to normal value immediately. In fact, their model slowly adjusts the determination of normal price to match the traded price thus taking into account persistence of sentiment which has influenced its value.

The algorithm for performing these evaluations is proprietary but the statistics are available for purchase from Value Line. Subscription terms are given in Appendix A.

SUMMARY OF WARRANT MODELS

The previous sections have examined some simple and some esoteric research regarding warrant models. The reaction to this exercise could easily be one of frustration and confusion. Using Sperry Rand warrants as an example, the various models do not converge on the actual price nor are they biased in any particular direction.

Sentiment, emotion, and perhaps other factors cause aberrations in the price of individual warrants as do broad secular changes in the warrant market as a whole. The "correct" price is not a number easy to zero in on. Value Line, for example, considers any warrant within plus or minus ten percent of their projected normal value to be fairly priced and not an aberration. Therefore, at any particular juncture, both relative and absolute warrant evaluations are of use. This is particularly true if the investor avoids warrants in general but operates only in issues selling at extremes, whether grossly undervalued or grossly overvalued.

STANDARDIZED PRICE CURVES

As indicated earlier, the Samuelson model has been adopted as the vehicle central to an investment approach. The model provides a single equation which can easily be solved to produce a family of curves representative of warrant tracks. The results of such an exercise are shown in Exhibit 6–13. Plots for W/E versus S/E are shown for gamma ranging from a low of 1.3 to a high of 6.0.

After calculating S/E and W/E for a particular warrant and determining its track, W/E can be found for *any other* S/E

EXHIBIT 6–13
Standardized Warrant Price Curves

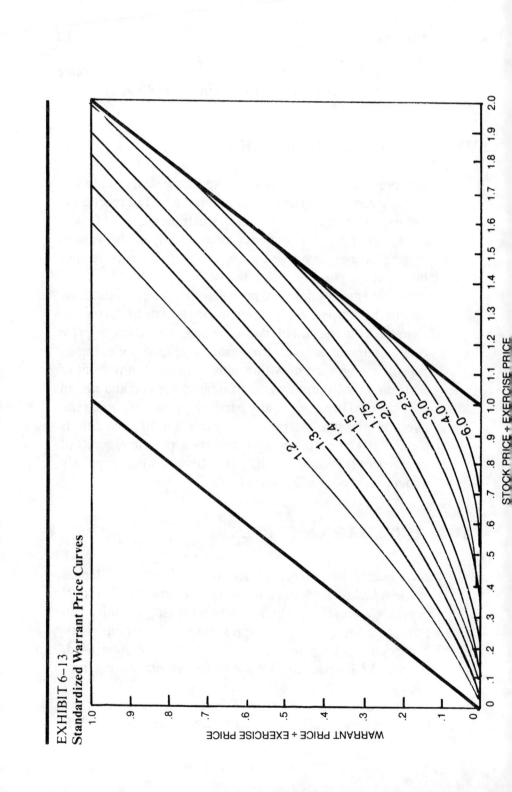

simply by reading the graph. Once W/E has been determined
the value of the traded warrant can be determined using the
following relationship:

$$\omega = (W/E) \times E \times n \qquad (6\text{--}23)$$

RISK REVISITED

In Chapter 4 the volatility of the underlying stock identified as
one of the primary factors determining the premium of a
warrant. However, in Chapter 4, volatility is defined only
briefly, but to evaluate warrants knowledgeable a greater understanding is necessary. The concept of volatility is profound
and the calculations for determining the factors are complex.
There is even debate about the proper methodology to be used.
Nevertheless, volatility is important, and a value must be established before the warrant evaluation process can proceed.

Standard Deviation

Volatility is a measure of a stock's propensity to change over a
period of time. It is generally computed from historical data—
weekly or daily prices going back as much as five years. More
precisely, volatility is a statistical calculation; namely, it is the
annualized standard deviation of security price changes.

Briefly, the process for determining volatility is as follows.
Security price changes are observed at regular intervals. A
frequency histogram is constructed and if enough observations
have been made, the outline of the histogram will assume the
characteristic bell-shaped curve so familiar in statistical stud-
ies. The standard deviation, which is a measure of the disper-
sion reflected by the curve, is then calculated. For low volatility stocks small price changes will occur with highest
occurrence. Thus, the bell-shaped curve will be narrow and
the standard deviation (volatility) will be small. For high
volatility stocks there is a greater incidence of large price
changes. Thus, the bell-shaped curve will be wide and the

standard deviation (volatility) will be large. The volatility of
the broad-based stock market indexes is about .20. The range in
standard deviation falls between .10 for low volatility stocks to
.95 for high volatility stocks.

Standard deviation can be interpreted as follows. If a stock
has an annualized standard deviation of .18, the stock will fall
within 18 percent of its current price, two years out of three.
While this definition is an oversimplification, it is adequate
for the purpose at hand.

Value Line Volatility[1]

Value Line, the investment advisory service, uses a variation
of the standard deviation approach for determining volatility.
Since one of their services (see Appendix A) gives in-depth
coverage of warrants many investors will find access to this
service essential. Since they provide the volatility statistics
for the stocks having warrants, it is appropriate to discuss
their methodology.

As is the case with most techniques for determining volatility, Value Line uses historical price data. Naturally, this procedure assumes that past volatility is an indication of future
volatility. Observations show that volatility tends to persist
over time so this type of calculation provides an acceptable
guide to the uncertainty that exists in predicting future prices.

Value Line identifies risk with uncertainty, and to quantify
this concept and to permit useful comparisons between alternative investments developed the concept of relative volatility. The relative volatility (RV) for a common stock is computed using the standard deviation (s.d.) of the natural log of
weekly percentage price changes of a security over a five-year
period. This calculation is performed for all 1700 common
stocks covered by Value Line. The median standard deviation is then assigned a RV of 100 percent. Using this s.d. as a
divisor, the RV of each stock is then computed.

[1] See Value Line Options & Convertibles, Part III: The Option Strategist,
Vol. 12 No. 7 (February 16, 1981).

Securities about as risky as the typical common stock have an RV of 100 percent (meaning 100 percent as risky as the typical common stock). Similarly, a RV of 50 percent means that the issue is about half as risky as the typical common stock. Finally, a RV of 200 percent means the issue is about twice as risky as the typical common stock.

Value Line updates the RV for every stock on a quarterly basis. Currently the raw s.d.—the median s.d. of the 1700 stocks monitored—is 4.7500. An issue with this s.d. is defined as having a volatility of 100 percent. A security with a RV of 110 percent would have a raw s.d. of 5.2250 (1.1 times 4.7500). Similarly, a RV of 90 percent would have a raw s.d. of 4.2750 (0.9 times 4.7500).

RAPID EVALUATION MATRIX

In the preceding chapters this book has identified the factors which influence a warrant's price and has given insight into the mathematics necessary to solve for fair warrant value provided these factors are known.

For most investors, calculation of a warrant's fair value to the nearest penny is not essential. Having an opinion about the underlying stock it is sufficient to know if the warrant is fairly valued and whether or not it is a superior alternative to the common stock. For investors equipped to capitalize on warrant mispricing, it is necessary to identify grossly undervalued or grossly overvalued issues. The hedging techniques described in Chapters 8 and 9 can then be employed.

A rapid means for determining a warrant's fair market value is given in Exhibit 6–14. This matrix gives the user the anticipated value of W/E when S/E = 1 provided the stock volatility, stock dividend, and warrant life are known. The matrix also provides the value of gamma for that particular point thus establishing the warrant's track. Once gamma is ascertained, the standardized price curves can be used to find W/E and thus W for the current value of S/E. This

EXHIBIT 6-14
Determining a Warrant's Fair Value and Track, Given Stock Volatility, Stock Yield, and Warrant Life

Value Line Volatility		50–100				100–150				150–200				200–250				250–300			
Annualized Std. Dev.		.18–.35				.35–.53				.53–.70				.70–.88				.88–1.05			
Expiration (Years)		4	3	2	1	4	3	2	1	4	3	2	1	4	3	2	1	4	3	2	1
SY= 0–4%	γ	2.28	2.36	2.56	2.97	1.76	1.85	2.00	2.28	1.51	1.56	1.69	1.89	1.34	1.39	1.47	1.65	1.23	1.28	1.35	1.49
	W/E at S/E=1	.21	.20	.18	.15	.30	.28	.25	.21	.38	.36	.32	.27	.47	.44	.40	.33	.55	.51	.46	.39
SY= 4–8%	γ	2.56	2.68	2.97	3.34	1.89	2.00	2.13	2.46	1.59	1.65	1.80	2.00	1.39	1.44	1.54	1.72	1.27	1.32	1.39	1.54
	W/E at S/E=1	.18	.17	.15	.13	.27	.25	.23	.19	.35	.33	.29	.25	.44	.41	.37	.31	.52	.48	.44	.37
SY= 8–12%	γ	2.82	2.97	3.34	3.86	2.06	2.20	2.36	2.68	1.62	1.69	1.80	2.06	1.44	1.51	1.62	1.80	1.29	1.34	1.42	1.59
	W/E at S/E=1	.16	.15	.13	.11	.24	.22	.20	.17	.34	.32	.29	.24	.41	.38	.34	.29	.50	.47	.42	.35
SY= 12–16%	γ	3.34	3.58	3.86	4.60	2.28	2.36	2.56	2.97	1.72	1.80	1.94	2.20	1.47	1.54	1.62	1.85	1.34	1.39	1.47	1.65
	W/E at S/E=1	.13	.12	.11	.09	.21	.20	.18	.15	.31	.29	.26	.22	.40	.37	.34	.28	.47	.44	.40	.33

SY = Stock Yield.

expected value can be compared with the warrant's actual value to determine whether or not mispricing exists.

Matrix Design

The primary inputs to the design of the matrix are empirical data. For example, the premium for a long life warrant on a volatile low-yielding stock normally is about 40 percent. This is one benchmark on the matrix. For warrants having a one year life, the Black-Scholes option model (corrected for dividends) is employed. For all practical purposes, a short term warrant and a listed option are equivalent, and the Black-Scholes model accurately prices such options. It is a common observation that warrants seldom enjoy additional premium as their life exceeds four years. It is also a fact that the warrant premium decays exponentialy with time. In constructing the matrix it was assumed that the one year estimates based on the Black-Scholes model were the most accurate. The four year level was set so that the exponential decay reduced the warrant to the Black-Scholes level at the one year point.

Using the Matrix

Use of the matrix is straightforward. The objective is to determine W/E for a warrant when S/E = 1. In conjunction with the standardized warrant price curves or equation (6-7), the modified Samuelson model, it is then possible to determine a warrant's track and project its price for any underlying stock price. The steps to be followed are as follows:

1. Collect the data critical in determining a warrant's price—namely, stock volatility, stock yield, and warrant life.
2. Enter the matrix to find W/E for the warrant when S/E = 1 as well as gamma for the particular issue. This identifies the warrant track.

3. Using the graph in Exhibit 6–13 find W/E at the proper level of gamma for the current S/E ratio.

4. The fair value for the traded warrant is:

$$\omega = (W/E) \times E \times n$$

This value can then be compared with the actual value of the warrant as it trades in the marketplace to give an indication of the amount by which it deviates from fair value.

5. A curve for a specific warrant can be calculated using equation (6–7) which is repeated below:

$$\omega = (E)(c - 1)\left(\frac{S}{cE}\right)^{\gamma}$$

CHAPTER
7

SPECULATING WITH WARRANTS

INTRODUCTION

The leverage which a warrant possesses permits spectacular gains when the underlying stock makes a major move. The impressiveness of these gains has been eclipsed recently because competitive fireworks now occur with great regularity in the option market. Nevertheless, a review of some historical winners (and losers) is interesting. Further, it should be remembered that warrants generally possess an important advantage over options—namely, longer life. Speculating with options requires that the stock advance within nine months or less. Otherwise the premium is lost. Warrant traders often have years for an investment to work out. The other important attribute of long life is the possibility of obtaining tax favored long term capital gains.

HISTORICAL EXAMPLES

Investment bankers, acting as underwriters, often receive warrants as partial compensation for their efforts in bringing new issues to market. These are generally private placements and the warrants are restricted issues; that is, they have no public market, and they cannot be readily transferred within a prescribed time limit. Information about the performance of these warrants over the long term is privy to the underwriters. However, given the spectacular performance of new issues in various phases of the market cycle, it can be surmised that the underwriters were rewarded handsomely.

The examples which follow give a small sample of the action to expect in the warrant market. The R.K.O. warrants and the Tri-Continental warrants were spectacular winners. They are old examples but they still appear in literature advertising warrant advisory services. The American and Foreign Power Company warrants, also an historical example, demonstrate the magnitude of the loss possible when the price action is unfavorable. The chapter concludes with a recent example, that of The Charter Company warrants. It illustrates vividly just how rapidly the fortunes of a business can change.

R.K.O. Warrants

One spectacular warrant often referred to in the literature is that of the R.K.O. Company. In the four-year period between 1942 and 1946 the stock advanced from a low of 2 1/2 to a high of 28. At the same time, the R.K.O. warrants advanced from 1/16 (6 1/4c) to 13. A $500 investment in the stock would have grown to $5600. The same $500 invested in the warrants would have grown to $104,000.

Tri-Continental Warrants

The advance in Tri-Continental warrants was even more phenomenal although the advance took somewhat longer.

They rose from a low of 1/32 (3 1/8c) in 1942 to a high of 75 3/4 in 1969.

American and Foreign Power Company Warrants

Less publicized are the dozens and dozens of warrants which have expired worthless providing holders with a loss of 100 percent. The American and Foreign Power Company Warrants, a 7,100,000 share issue, traded at a peak price of 175 in 1929 for a market value in excess of one billion dollars. Following adverse circumstances, the company was recapitalized in 1952, but the new structure did not include the warrants and the entire issue had to be written off as worthless. Indeed, dealing with warrants can be a treacherous affair.

ECLIPSE BY LISTED OPTIONS

Movements of the magnitude demonstrated in the preceding examples were once confined almost exclusively to the warrant markets. However, listed options now provide a competitive investment with similar characteristics—in particular, leverage. Large percentage increases in a very short time period occur frequently, and because the financial community and the press pay particular attention to options markets, these spectacular examples are generally well publicized. For example in September 1984, on reports that a group headed by former Esmark officers would buy out the company, the Northwest Industries September 50 call option rose from 1/16 to 11 1/4, a phenomenal 17,900 percent. It is no wonder that options in general and warrants in particular retain their speculative appeal.

CASE STUDY: THE CHARTER COMPANY WARRANTS

Of course it is no revelation that stocks make wild gyrations and that warrants on these issues follow suit. However, one additional example will be explored. It is of particular interest because the terms of the issue gave the purchaser an additional element of protection. The discussion also shows a detailed analysis of the type which should be performed prior to entering a situation.

Terms and Statistics

The Charter Company warrants were issued September 28, 1978 accompanying a Charter Company subordinated debenture, the 10 5/8s of 1998. Basic information about the securities is given in Exhibit 7-1. The warrant had some special provisions as well. The expiration could be accelerated to as early as September 1, 1983 if the common closed 120 percent above the exercise price for 60 consecutive trading days. In addition, the warrants could be tendered to Charter Company for $1.25 each in cash, at the holder's option, during the ten trading days ending September 1, 1983 and again, if the expiration date had not been accelerated, during the 10 trading days ending September 1, 1988. In essence the warrant had an option attached enabling the holder to put the warrant to the company under certain very restricted conditions.

Trading began on the New York stock exchange the following week with the stock at 6 and the warrant at 1 1/2. Considering the put feature, it appeared that initial investors had very limited risk exposure.

Analysis of Indicators

The value indicators for The Charter Company warrant are given in Exhibit 7-2 and the position of the warrant on the warrant diagram is shown in Exhibit 7-3. The warrant is low in the diagram especially in view of the fact that it makes no adjustment for the put feature. The various indicators are satisfactory but not outstanding.

EXHIBIT 7–1
Security Statistics
The Charter Company
Industry Group: Petroleum Integrated
October 1978

Common Stock		Warrant	
Price	6	Price	$1\frac{1}{2}$
Volatility	140%	Exercise price	10
Dividend	$.24	Effective exercise price	8.90
52-Week high	8	Conversion Ratio	1.000
52-Week low	$3\frac{3}{4}$	Expiration	9-01-88
S&P Rank	B+	Time remaining	10 years
		Issue size	3,750,000

Usable Bond	
Issue	$10\frac{5}{8}$s of 1998
Price	89
Issue size	$50,000,000
S&P Rank	B
Current yield	11.9%
Maturity	9-01-98
Yield-to-maturity	12.1%

EXHIBIT 7–2
Value Indicators
The Charter Company Warrants
October 1978

Gamma Factor (γ)	1.668
Normalized Stock Price (S/E)	0.67
Normalized Warrant Price (W/E)	0.17
Premium (P1)	25.0
Premium (P2)	73.3
Leverage Indicator (LI)	4.0
Leverage Ratio (LR)	2.2
Mathematical Advantage (MA)	1.6
Appreciation Multiple (M1)	9.8
Appreciation Multiple (M2)	2.0

EXHIBIT 7–3
**The Charter Company Warrants Position
in the Warrant Diagram at Selected Intervals**

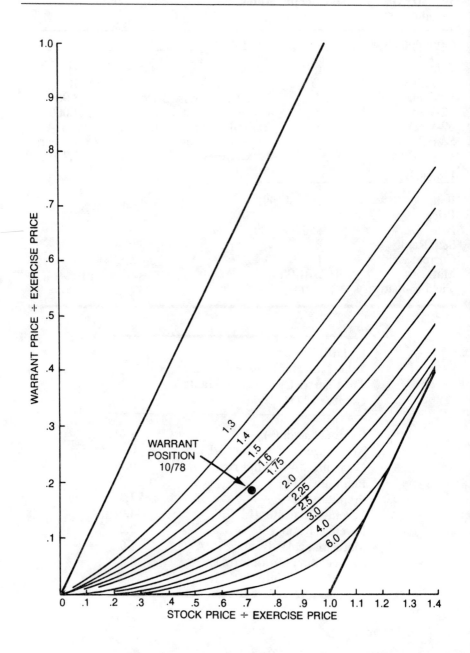

Trading History

A price chart for The Charter Company stock and warrant from October 1978 through December 1984 is given in Exhibit 7–4. Shortly after listing, the warrant traded as low as 1 from which point it soared to a high of 45 3/4 in slightly less than one year. This represents a gain of 4,475 percent. However, troubles were developing within the company, which the market perceived at the time, and the stock and warrant began a gradual and persistent decline. In April 1984 the company filed for bankruptcy. At the time the stock was 3 1/2 and the warrants were trading around 1 1/2.

Subsequently the stock and warrant dropped even lower. Just what value the put feature will have when the next window for exercise opens in 1988 is definitely a matter of conjecture. It appears that no matter how attractive the terms, every investment has potential for severe disappointment. The Charter warrant also illustrates the other problem always facing investors: How high is high? Seeing a price history in retrospect—a move from 1 1/2 to 45 3/4 and back

EXHIBIT 7–4
The Charter Company Securities Price History

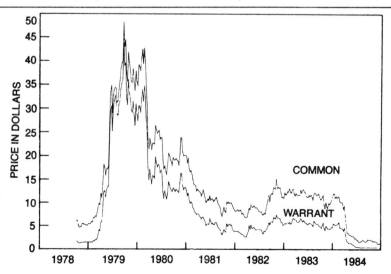

EXHIBIT 7–5	
Value Indicators	
The Charter Company Warrants	
September 1979	
Gamma Factor (γ)	1.037
Normalized Stock Price (S/E)	5.36
Normalized Warrant Price (W/E)	4.86
Premium (P1)	9.3
Premium (P2)	9.3
Leverage Indicator (LI)	1.1
Leverage Ratio (LR)	1.1
Mathematical Advantage (MA)	1.0
Appreciation Multiple (M1)	11.2
Appreciation Multiple (M2)	2.0

to 1/2—tells little about how the investor would have handled the situation as the prices unfolded.

The value indicators near the peak are given in Exhibit 7–5. Of course, the indicators show substantial deterioration because the warrant moved well in-the-money. Nevertheless, the warrant still possessed premium, a fact which can only be explained by the ignorance of the speculators.

PURCHASE CRITERIA

As is the case with most options, warrants usually give more bang for the buck when the underlying security advances. Traders with conviction are usually ahead by selecting warrants as the vehicle in which to operate. Investors with a longer time horizon, however, may find the warrant to be unacceptable under any circumstances. The following guidelines list the important factors to consider before committing funds to warrants for the long term:

1. Give appropriate consideration to the fundamentals of the underlying stock. If the common is unacceptable as a portfolio holding the warrant is generally unacceptable also.

2. Buy undervalued warrants if possible. Otherwise restrict purchases to fairly valued warrants and avoid overvalued warrants. If the investor is consistently above average in selecting stocks, these rules will enhance performance. Purchasing overvalued warrants may cause losses if the common declines, remains unchanged, or even advances.

3. Give the investment time to work out. Buy issues having a remaining life of at least two and preferably three years. The warrant is a wasting asset, and time is the enemy of warrant holders. A year evaporates quickly and, if the warrant does not have sufficient life when purchased, it may enter the zone of accelerated price depreciation before the investor's hoped-for advance occurs.

4. Read the footnotes. Be aware of any special features which may influence the warrant's price. For example, some warrants are callable at a specified price. The issuer may exercise this privilege to force conversion; however, the warrants will fall to intrinsic value as an outcome.

5. Avoid takeover situations. Assume an offer of cash is made and accepted for the shares of a company and the agreed upon price is less than the exercise price of the warrants. The warrant becomes an option to buy a fixed dollar amount of cash by submitting an amount equal to the exercise price which is even higher; in other words, the warrant becomes worthless. Although warrant holders have received special compensation in some instances, they have also been short-changed in others, and the risk is not acceptable.

6. Integrate warrants into a portfolio maintained in accordance with traditional prudent investment practice. In other words, diversify and do not permit a single issue to represent an inordinate amount of the portfolio.

CHAPTER

8

HEDGING I: WARRANT LONG POSITIONS

INTRODUCTION

Chapters 8 and 9 explore warrant hedges; that is, warrant positions in combination with other securities. The emphasis in this chapter is on undervalued warrants used in conjunction with the sale of call options or common stock. This combination is known as a *convertible hedge* because the warrants can always be exercised (converted into stock) to offset the short position. Chapter 9 explores the opposite type of hedge; that is, the sale of overvalued warrants in conjunction with the purchase of common stock (or an equity-linked security). That combination is frequently referred to as a *reverse warrant hedge*.

FUNDAMENTAL CONCEPTS

Undervalued warrants, although worthy of consideration as a portfolio holding, are nevertheless extremely risky. A hedge is the mechanism whereby the investor can exploit the undervalued issues to enhance performance while at the same time controlling the risk. In fact, depending upon the securities used and the ratio of the long position to the short position, the risk can be tailored over a wide range to suit an investor's preference. Since there is no free lunch, the tradeoff is decreased expected return.

Although a warrant's price is intimately tied to the price of the underlying common, there is a degree of price independence as well. Most noteworthy is the tendency for the warrant to lag the common in major price swings. If the stock price plunges precipitously, the warrant often drops at a more casual pace. Similarly, if the common advances sharply, it often takes considerable time for the enthusiasm to spill over into the warrant sector.

Many other factors can be described which distort the supply/demand balance between the common and the warrant. The important message is that pricing inefficiencies occur regularly, and they provide the knowledgeable and alert investor additional candidates for diversifying a portfolio.

SELECTION CRITERIA

The kingpin of the convertible warrant hedge is a grossly undervalued warrant. Generally these are flagged by the advisory services specializing in warrants. The investor can also identify these situations by maintaining historical price records and comparing the stock/warrant price relationship with the warrant's normal value curve.

The warrant should have more than three years of life

remaining. The warrant is a wasting asset, and as expiration approaches decay of the time premium will interfere with the profit projections. When hedging with stock, only low yielding issues should be considered. The seller is liable for dividends on short positions, and the relentless debiting of large quarterly payments can ultimately destroy the potential of even the most promising hedge.

Generally convertible hedges are designed to capitalize on an upswing while protecting against loss in the event of a stock decline. Only these bullish hedges will be discussed here. However, less optimistic investors can adjust the hedge ratio so that the profit profile is neutral or even bearish.

SHORTING STOCKS OR OPTIONS

In its classic form the warrant convertible hedge is constructed using common stock for the short position. However if options are available for the underlying common, the hedge outcome may be superior if calls are sold rather than stock.

No formulas have been derived to determine how much stock or how many options should be sold short in conjunction with a given warrant position. Selecting the long/short ratio is basically an iterative process. The outcomes for various ratios are examined until an acceptable profit profile is obtained. The short position is increased until the investor is satisfied with the downside protection received in exchange for the upside potential sacrificed.

CASE STUDY: WARNER COMMUNICATIONS WARRANTS

The Warner Communications warrants were issued in January 1981, the result of a special distribution to shareholders, and trading was instituted immediately on the American Stock Exchange. Additional warrants were issued in February of that year in conjunction with a major acquisition. Since it first appeared, this warrant offered several different trading opportunities which will be analyzed in this chapter and chapter 9.

After the warrant was issued, the company's fortunes ebbed and flowed and the stock price gyrated accordingly. On most occasions the warrant tracked the stock, but there were several instances when the warrant was relatively cheap or dear. Such price alignments produced some very interesting investment opportunities.

Stock/Warrant Price History

Exhibit 8-1 is a price history for Warner Communications stock (ticker symbol WCI) and warrants from the period of original issue in 1981 through December 1984. At first examination three facts are immediately clear. First, WCI is a volatile stock. Large price excursions occur frequently. Second, the warrant tracks the common but the correlation is not

EXHIBIT 8-1
Warner Communications
Securities Price History

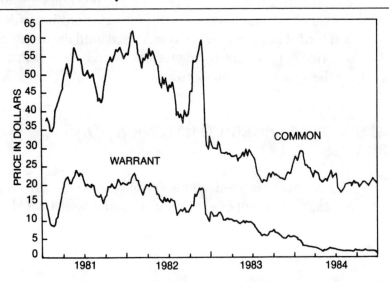

perfect. Third, there is a persistent and relentless decay in the warrant premium as time progresses.

In early 1981 the stock advanced sharply but the warrant did not appreciate proportionately. At that time the recommended strategy was to purchase the warrant or, because its volatility was probably unacceptable to most investors, to hedge long positions with stock or call options. The opportunity to close that hedge came swiftly as the normal warrant/stock relationship returned within a month.

In January 1981 Warner Communications common stock traded above $40 and the warrant changed hands above $15. In late February 1981 the common dropped to $34, a decline of 15 percent. At the same time the warrant plunged precipitously, dropping to $8, a decline of nearly 47 percent.

The alert investor should be sensitive to such disproportionate price swings. They suggest that selling in the warrant is overdone and that a true bargain may have developed. The

EXHIBIT 8–2
Warner Communications Warrants
Normal Value Curve

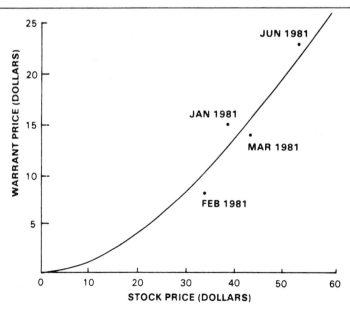

which would apply to the typical long term warrant for a volatile low yielding stock. Plotted on the curve are four points showing the warrant/stock price relationship in the period under consideration. In January 1981 at the time of issue, the warrant was considerably above the curve. One month later in February 1981, the warrant traded considerably below its normal value curve. This was the signal suggesting further analysis. Statistics for the various Warner Communications securities which might be incorporated into an investment strategy are given in Exhibit 8–3. The value indicators—that is, the various figures of merit developed in Chapter 5—are presented in Exhibit 8–4.

EXHIBIT 8–3
Security Statistics
Warner Communications
Industry Group: Entertainment
February 1981

Common Stock		Warrant	
Price	$34	Price	$ 8
Volatility	100%	Exercise price	$55
Beta	1.20	Conversion ratio	1.000
52-week high	$42\frac{3}{4}$	Expiration	4-30-86
52-week low	$17\frac{3}{8}$	Remaining life	5.25 years
Dividend	$0.68	Issue size	3,663,000
S&P rank	A –		

Call Option	
Series	Aug 40
Price	$2
Expiration	8-22-81

EXHIBIT 8–4
Value Indicators
Warner Communications Warrants
February 1981

Gamma Factor (γ)	1.669
Normalized Stock Price (S/E)	0.62
Normalized Warrant Price (W/E)	0.15
Premium (P1)	23.5
Premium (P2)	85.3
Leverage Indicator (LI)	4.3
Leverage Ratio (LR)	2.2
Mathematical Advantage (MA)	1.6
Appreciation Multiple (M1)	21.2
Appreciation Multiple (M2)	2.1

Warrant/Stock Hedge

Exhibit 8–5 is a worksheet showing profit profile calculations for a warrant position hedged with common stock sold short. For this example it was assumed that 1,000 warrants were purchased. The short position, 300 shares of common, was selected through trial and error until the the hedge outcome produced a favorable risk/reward tradeoff. In this configuration the bottom line shows that, even after commissions, the hedge had much of the potential of the stock at a fraction of the exposure to loss.

As explained earlier, WCI did make a good price advance. By March 1981 the warrant had returned to its normal value curve and liquidation of the hedge was indicated. The stock moved from 34 to 43 and the warrant advanced from 8 to 14. Especially gratifying was the fact that the move occurred swiftly. The outcome was essentially as predicted on the worksheet, a return exceeding 30 percent after commissions on a position entailing minimal risk. Had one been perfectly clairvoyant, the hedge would have been retained until June 1981 when the warrant once again became overpriced.

EXHIBIT 8–5
Warrant/Stock Hedge
Warner Communications
February 1981

Position (unleveraged)

Buy 1,000 WCI warrants at 8.00	=	$ 8,000
Sell 300 WCI common at 34.00	=	10,200
Commissions	=	415
Net Investment	=	$ 8,415

Risk/Reward Analysis (assuming 6-month holding period)

	-25%	0	$+25\%$	$+50\%$
Stock price change	-25%	0	$+25\%$	$+50\%$
Stock price	$25\frac{1}{2}$	34	$42\frac{1}{2}$	51
Estimated warrant price	$6\frac{1}{4}$	8	$14\frac{1}{2}$	19
Profit (loss) warrant	(1,750)	0	6,500	11,000
Profit (loss) stock	2,550	0	(2,550)	(5,100)
Dividends paid	(102)	(102)	(102)	(102)
Commissions	(780)	(415)*	(950)	(1,035)
Net profit	(82)	(517)	2,898	4,763
Percent return for 6 months	-1.0%	-6.1%	$+34.4\%$	$+56.6\%$

*Closing commissions are not included as it is assumed the undervalued warrant would be retained in the hedge.

Warrant/Option Hedge

Exhibit 8–6 is a worksheet showing profit profile calculations for a warrant position hedged with call options. The prices are the same as those used in the previous example. The sale of 7 August 40 call options for each 1,000 warrants purchased provided substantial protection in the event of a stock price decline without sacrificing too much of the warrant's potential on the upside.

The outcome for the warrant/option hedge was similar to that for the warrant/stock hedge—a return of approximately 21 percent. This value is somewhat less than the worksheet

EXHIBIT 8-6
Warrant/Option Hedge
Warner Communications
February 1981

Position (unleveraged)

Buy 1,000 WCI warrants at 8.00	=	$	8,000
Sell 5 WCI Aug 35 calls at 3.50	=		1,750
Commissions	=		305
Net Investment	=	$	6,555

Risk/Reward Analysis (6-month holding period)

Stock price change	– 25%	0	+ 25%	+ 50%
Stock price	25½	34	42½	51
Estimated warrant price	6¼	8	14½	19
Estimated call price	0	0	7½	16
Profit (loss) warrant	(1,750)	0	6,500	11,000
Profit (loss) call options	1,750	1,750	(2,000)	(6,250)
Commissions	(510)	(305)*	(720)	(825)
Net profit	(510)	1,445	3,780	3,925
Percentage return for 6 months	– 7.8%	– 22.0%	+ 57.7%	+ 59.9%

*Closing commissions on the securities held long are not included in the calculations as it is assumed they will be held for hedging with future options.

projection because the warrant returned to its normal value, and the hedge was terminated prior to expiration of the call option. (Had the warrant remained undervalued it would have been retained until the options expired when the sale of additional options would have been considered). Since the call was not close to expiration it retained considerable speculative premium. It was closed at a price of 9 1/2 rather than at the 7 1/2 level shown on the worksheet. This accounts for the difference in actual and projected returns with the stock price in the vicinity of 43.

The profit profiles (that is, the projected return on investment for various stock prices at a future time) are quite different. They exhibit characteristics in common, however. Both provide relatively low exposure to loss in the event of a major drop in the common, and both provide a handsome return in a rising stock scenario.

There is not necessarily an optimum approach. Depending upon the level of option premiums, one hedge may be clearly superior to the other. The final selection, however, is best determined by investor preference and perception of the future stock price level.

MARGIN REQUIREMENTS

There is an interesting provision in the margin regulations pertaining to convertible securities (including warrants). If a convertible is held in an account, common stock can be sold short up to the full amount into which the convertible can be exchanged without posting additional margin. Thus, having purchased 1,000 WCI warrants (either for cash or on margin), up to 1,000 shares of common stock could be sold short without additional collateral.

Options written against warrants (or any other convertible) are considered covered. The proceeds of the sale are available immediately and reduce the investment required for the hedge. If the required collateral is available for the warrants, no additional collateral is required to sell the options.

POSSIBLE PITFALLS

Not every undervalued warrant is a good hedge candidate. There are several possible pitfalls and screening of many factors is essential before committing funds. While the potential problems may seem prohibitive, they do not preclude the warrant hedge as a viable investment. A small amount of research and a knowledge of markets prior to entry will permit investment success.

Expanding Undervaluation

The normal value curves are not rails along which the warrant must track as the common makes price excursions. Given that a warrant is undervalued does not guarantee that it will return shortly to its fair value. In fact, it may become more undervalued in the future. This problem is minimized if investment is restricted to grossly undervalued situations. In addition, when making warrant price projections and selecting hedge ratios, a conservative approach is advised. Assume, for example, that the warrant will remain undervalued throughout the duration of the investment. Hedge positions with undervalued warrants have excellent potential for appreciation even if the warrant remains undervalued.

Approaching Expiration

A warrant is a wasting asset, and the premium decay usually begins in earnest three to four years prior to the expiration date. The passage of time works to the warrant holder's disadvantage. To be profitable the warrant must return to its fair value, or the common must make a major price move within a relatively short time span. Otherwise, the premium loss will be impossible to overcome and retention of the warrant would be of dubious value. Warrants selected for hedging should have a lifetime exceeding three years.

Merger Activity

Whenever a warrant purchase is contemplated, the issuer should be evaluated as a potential takeover candidate. If there are merger rumors or negotiations, or if other corporate investors are holding large blocks of the underlying stock, the warrant should be avoided. A corporate suitor, while generous to shareholders, may be less than fair to warrant holders. For example, in an acquisition for cash which happens to be below the warrant's exercise price, the warrant is rendered

worthless. Warrant holders are at the mercy of the acquiring
company, and the record shows that benevolence has been the
exception rather than the rule. Warrant holders have incurred
large losses in such situations.

Short Sales

When hedging undervalued warrants with stock a short sale
is required, and all the obstacles introduced by this procedure
come into play. For example, short sales must be executed on
an uptick. Thus it may be difficult to establish a hedge when
the market is declining. Another difficulty associated with
short selling is borrowing the shares and maintaining the
position. However, the common stock issue is generally large,
very liquid, and seldom in tight supply. The brokerage firms
also monitor their inventory of stock carefully so that a
buy-in, an unwanted repurchase of stock sold short, is seldom
encountered.

High Stock Dividend

When hedging warrants with common stock, there is a dividend liability for the short sale, and the stock yield must be
subtracted from the total return when the risk/reward analysis is prepared. However, even if the profit profile is satisfactory, it is wise to avoid shorting stocks with large dividends. If
the stock price remains unchanged, the return on the hedge is
negative. A year's time elapses quickly, the dividends are
debited relentlessly, and the losses accumulate rapidly.

Coincidental Executions

The inveterate hedger considers any position without its corresponding offset to be rank speculation. However, although
hedging eliminates many problems it introduces others. For
example, small differences in the initial prices can have a

significant impact on the outcome of the hedge. Therefore, extreme care must be exercised when entering the positions. If stock is used, the short should be executed first because of the problems associated with this type of order.

With a little work and perseverance, valuable information is available to assist in implementing a hedge. Markets should be checked prior to placing orders by obtaining *quote and size* information. The *quote* component gives the bid and asked prices for the securities involved and thereby reveals the price spread. The *size* component indicates the number of shares which can be purchased or sold at the indicated prices. Of course the process should be repeated when exiting or undoing the hedge.

SUMMARY

Most of the time most warrants are fairly priced. They are high risk securities which will produce high returns in a diversified portfolio managed by a disciplined investor.

Occasionally, however, market forces cause distortion of the normal warrant-stock relationship, and warrant prices become unreasonably cheap or dear with respect to the stock. Unusually cheap warrants should be purchased or hedged with stock or call options. Unusually dear warrants should not be retained, and short sales (especially hedged) should be considered.

This chapter explored the ramifications of purchasing undervalued warrants. Chapter 9 addresses overpriced warrants and the considerations involved in selling warrants short.

CHAPTER

9

HEDGING II: WARRANT SHORT POSITIONS

INTRODUCTION

Undervalued warrants are exploited through carefully directed purchasing programs and risk is tailored to the investor's preference through hedging strategies. Overvalued warrants can be exploited in a similar manner. The classic strategy is a hedge involving the sale of expiring warrants in conjunction with the purchase of common stock.

REVERSE WARRANT HEDGES

The basic strategy is straightforward. Common stock is purchased, and overpriced expiring warrants are sold short. The objective is to capture the premium of the warrant without being exposed to the high risk that an outright short sale of the warrant would entail. When the number of warrants sold short equals the number of shares of stock purchased, the hedge is similar to covered call writing. When the number of warrants sold exceeds the number of shares long the hedge is similar to variable call writing.

The number of warrants shorted compared to the number of common shares purchased is called the hedge ratio. Exhibit 9–1 is a generalized diagram showing the hedge outcome as this ratio is varied. Increasing the ratio has three effects: it lowers the downside breakeven point, it lowers the upside breakeven point, and it increases the return in the case where the stock is at the exercise price when the warrant expires.

There is no simple rule for determining the hedge ratio. A 3:1 ratio is frequently a good starting point. The profit profiles of other ratios should then be examined until the possible returns coupled with the cushion on the upside and downside suit the investor's needs. In calculating the profit profiles it is helpful to know that they are always triangular in shape (except when the hedge ratio is 1:1), that the maximum profit always occurs at the exercise price, and that the profiles have a common intersection. Two simple formulas assist in rapid

EXHIBIT 9–1
Affect of Hedge Ratio Changes on the Profit Profile

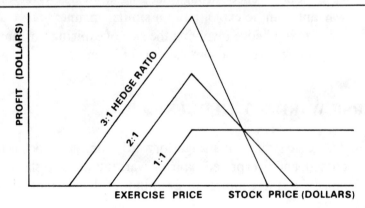

determination of the upside and downside breakeven points:

$$A = S - RW \qquad (9\text{--}1)$$

$$B = \frac{R(W + E) - S}{R - 1} \qquad (9\text{--}2)$$

where A = downside breakeven   S = stock price
       B = upside breakeven   W = warrant price
       R = hedge ratio   E = exercise price

CASE STUDY: WARNER COMMUNICATIONS WARRANTS

Exhibit 9–2 is repeated from Chapter 8. It is a price history for Warner Communications stock and warrants from the period of original issue in January 1981 through December 1984. Beginning in December 1982, and continuing for several months thereafter, the Warner Communications warrants aligned to produce an outstanding reverse hedge. The

EXHIBIT 9–2
Warner Communications
Securities Price History

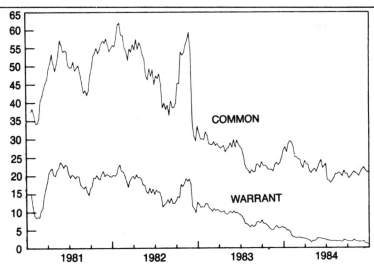

common stock experienced extreme selling pressure as unanticipated bad news unfolded and insiders (corporate executives), as well as the public, liquidated shares with abandon. The warrant price, although sharply lower, did not fall as much as might be anticipated under the circumstances.

The statistics for the stock and the warrant at this juncture are given in Exhibit 9–3 and the value indicators in Exhibit 9–4. The position of the warrant with respect to the normal value curve is shown in Exhibit 9–5. The warrant was overvalued, the primary requirement for a successful hedge, and the impending expiration insured that the warrant would be forced to its intrinsic value within a known time frame thereby insuring that the overvaluation would disappear.

A preliminary analysis showing the lower and upper breakeven points and the maximum profit for various hedge ratios is given in Exhibit 9–6. From these data a hedge ratio of 2:1 was selected for further investigation because it provided protection well in excess of price extremes anticipated for WCI common prior to expiration of the warrant. A detailed

---

EXHIBIT 9–3
Security Statistics
Warner Communications
Industry Group: Recreation
December 1982

Common Stock		Warrant	
Price	30	Price	10
Volatility	95%	Exercise price	55.00
Beta	1.05	Conversion ratio	1.000
52-week high	$63\frac{1}{4}$	Expiration	4-30-86
52-week low	27	Remaining life	3.36 years
Dividend	$1.00	Issue size	3,663,000
S&P rank	A –	52-week high	$23\frac{3}{4}$
		52-week low	$8\frac{7}{8}$

EXHIBIT 9–4
Value Indicators
Warner Communications Warrants
December 1982

Gamma Factor (γ)	1.410
Normalized Stock Price (S/E)	0.55
Normalized Warrant Price (W/E)	0.18
Premium (P1)	33.3
Premium (P2)	116.7
Leverage Indicator (LI)	3.0
Leverage Ratio (LR)	1.7
Mathematical Advantage (MA)	1.3
Appreciation Multiple (M1)	52.1
Appreciation Multiple (M2)	2.8

EXHIBIT 9–5
Warner Communications Warrants
Normal Value Curve

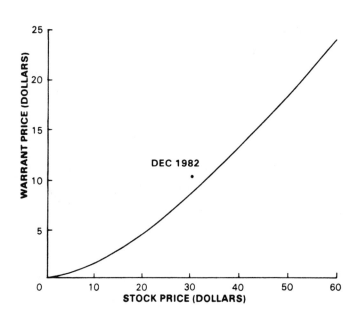

EXHIBIT 9–6
Profit Profiles for Various Hedge Ratios

Hedge Ratio	Lower Breakeven	Upper Breakeven	Maximum Profit
1	20	00[1]	$3,500
2	10	100	4,500
3	0	83	5,500
4	0[2]	77	6,500

[1]The profit profile is horizontal and thus never enters negative territory.
[2]A profit occurs if the stock price is $0. True breakeven would be at a hypothetical − $10.

EXHIBIT 9–7
Reverse Warrant Hedge
Warner Communications
December 1982

Position
Buy 1,000 WCI common at 30.00	=	$30,000
Sell 2,000 WCI warrants at 10.00	=	20,000
Commissions	=	920
Net Investment	=	$30,920

Risk/Reward Analysis
Assumed stock price	10	30	55	100
Estimated warrant price	0	0	0	45
Profit (loss) stock	(20,000)	0	25,000	70,000
Profit (loss) warrant	20,000	20,000	20,000	(70,000)
Income received	3,500	3,500	3,500	3,500
Margin interest	0	0	0	0
Commissions	(1,170)	(1,395)	(1,535)	(2,675)
Total gain (loss)	2,330	22,105	46,965	825
Return on investment	7.5%	71.5%	151.9%	2.7%
Annualized ROI (3.36 years)	2.2%	21.3%	45.2%	0.1%

analysis of the 2:1 reverse hedge, including dividends and commissions, is given in Exhibit 9–7 and the resulting profit profile is shown graphically in Exhibit 9–8.

MARGIN REQUIREMENTS

A reverse hedge can be executed on margin. To calculate the required margin each part of the hedge is treated as a separate unrelated transaction. Minimum initial margin is 50 percent of the net of each transaction or, excluding commissions, $15,000 for the stock plus $10,000 for the warrants for a total of $25,000. However, no debit balance is created; that is, the position is unleveraged if an amount equal to the full purchase price of the common plus total commissions is deposited. In this example all calculations are based on an unleveraged position.

EXHIBIT 9–8
Warner Communications Reverse Hedge
2:1 Hedge Ratio

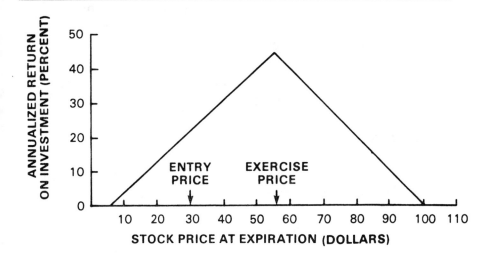

HEDGE OUTCOME

The hefty premium in the WCI warrants remained for approximately a full year. In late 1983 and early 1984, however, the premium began its inevitable contraction. At the time of this writing (March 1984) the stock was trading at the 23 level with the warrants near 2 1/2. Before commissions, this represents a $7,000 loss on the common and a $15,000 profit on the warrants.

When a hedge matures nicely as this one has done, the investor has several options. The hedge should be re-evaluated in terms of its remaining potential. If the hedge is attractive as a new position it should be retained, perhaps with adjustment of the hedge ratio. Otherwise, closing the hedge should be considered. There is no harm in nailing down profits. In addition, remaining with a reverse warrant hedge until expiration exposes the investment to some otherwise avoidable problems.

POSSIBLE PITFALLS

Every investment has special problems and unique difficulties. Reverse warrant hedging, like convertible warrant hedging, is no exception. With reverse hedges the most frequent sources of discomfort are associated with establishing and maintaining the short position or with extensions of the warrant expiration date.

Warrant Short Sales

To sell short means to sell borrowed shares. Generally a position can be entered and maintained as long as desired. Occasionally, however, the supply of securities to borrow becomes depleted. If at that time the original owners of the securities demand their certificates, the brokerage firm may be required to purchase some of the shares which had been shorted to make delivery. This is known as a *buy-in* and when it is necessary the client has no recourse.

Brokerage firms are usually able to maintain a short position once established. If the supply gets tight they disallow shorting of additional shares. Further, experience with a large number of short positions indicates that forced covering is not encountered frequently. Nevertheless, the risk is real.

Expiration Date Extensions

As a result of changes in the tax law, the period between 1972 and 1984 was a time when the expiration date of a warrant was subject to considerable uncertainty. Prior to April 24, 1972, warrant expirations were routine. The expiration date is a provision of the warrant agreement and there was ample precedent that warrants in-the-money were exercised and warrants out-of-the-money expired worthless.

Until 1972 there were no tax consequences to issuers of warrants if the warrants expired unexercised. However, the law was revised such that if warrants expired unexercised, the proceeds from the original sale of the warrants became taxable as ordinary income to the issuer in the year the warrants expired. Effective July 18, 1984, the tax code regarding this matter was changed again. Currently, a corporation does not recognize gain or loss on any lapse or repurchase of a warrant it issued to acquire its stock.

For many corporations, the tax liability incurred when a warrant expired unexercised was unacceptable and the technique used to escape the problem was simply to extend the life of the warrant. This was done in defiance of exchange objections and in violation of provisions of the warrant agreement. Nevertheless, extend they did and numerous examples are in the records. During the twelve-year period between 1972 and 1984 there was a considerable element of uncertainty in the reverse hedge strategy. Which warrants would be extended could not be predicted reliably. Some which were extension candidates never materialized. Others were affected by special considerations, such as earnings losses, so that the tax was not a consideration.

Most warrants issued between 1972 and 1984 had special provisions which permitted the issuer to force exercise before expiration when the warrant was out-of-the-money. One technique was to have the warrant automatically converted into a token amount of common—generally 1/100 or 1/200 of a share at expiration. The second technique was a provision permitting the issuer to lower the exercise price. This would put the warrant in-the-money and force exercise if the warrant were expiring.

SUMMARY

Warrants are complex securities, poorly understood by most investors. However attractive investments appear regularly and are worthy of the time it takes to study and follow the markets. The investor's objective should be to appreciate fully the potential of warrant hedges and to be alert for the occasional opportunities in mispricing as they arise.

CHAPTER
10

LATENT WARRANTS AND SYNTHETIC CONVERTIBLES

INTRODUCTION

Many financial instruments can be analyzed as options, and it is a trend in current research to apply option theory whenever possible. One of the first instruments recognized as having the features of an option is the convertible bond. Indeed, convertibles are nothing more than straight corporate debt with warrants attached. One of the best ways of understanding convertibles is to break them down into the component parts and to analyze each separately.

Similarly, convertibles can be fabricated; that is, created from the component parts. Because both halves of the synthetic instrument can be purchased and sold separately, they have certain advantages over conventional convertibles. Because the warrant is non-detachable from the debt portion of a conventional convertible, its value is usually less than might have been predicted using the standard warrant evaluation tools.

ANATOMY OF A CONVERTIBLE BOND

A convertible bond is a debt instrument with a special provision that it can be exchanged for other securities—usually a common stock issue—at the holder's option. Thus, the convertible is a hybrid security having characteristics of both debt and equity. The debt feature provides fixed income. The coupon on the bond is set at the time of the underwriting, and the interest is guaranteed unless the company goes into bankruptcy. Another feature of debt instruments is the existence of a final maturity date. At that time a predetermined amount is returned to the holder of the instrument. The conversion feature provides equity participation. Because of the option to convert into common, if the stock rises the convertible bond will also rise in price.

To fully understand a convertible security two concepts must be clear: that of investment value and that of conversion value. Once these concepts have been grasped the logic of stripping away the warrant from the straight bond portion of the convertible for separate analysis will be evident. Some of the evaluation techniques explained in the earlier chapters can be applied to the stripped warrants. Determining the cheapness or dearness of the warrant permits a determination of the fairness of the convertible's price.

Investment Value

Consider a straight debt instrument (not convertible) having a ten percent coupon and a 20-year life. With long term interest rates at 16 percent the bond would have to trade at a price of about $650 to provide a 16 percent yield to maturity competitive with other debt instruments of similar quality in the mar-

ketplace. New bonds coming to market would have a 16 percent coupon and would be priced at approximately $1,000.

The concept of investment value for a convertible bond
having a 10 percent coupon and a 20 year life is shown in
Exhibit 10–1. If non-convertible, the required yield to maturity would be 16 percent which means that the bond would be
priced at about $650 (65 percent of par). That price is called
the investment floor, and it is the approximate level below
which the convertible price would not be expected to fall.

In the real world this floor will fluctuate. Exhibit 10–2
shows how the investment value will vary with changes in the
long term interest rate. Other factors influence the floor as
well. With falling interest rates, elapsed time (as the bond
approaches maturity), or an improved outlook for the company or industry (implying a rise in the quality of the instrument), the floor will rise. Likewise, if there is a deteriorating
financial condition or if interest rates rise, the investment floor
will fall.

EXHIBIT 10–1
**Investment Value for a Hypothetical Convertible Bond Having
a 10 Percent Coupon and Maturing in 20 Years**

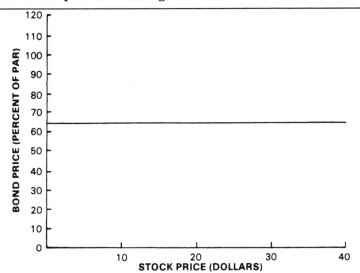

EXHIBIT 10–2
Price of a 10 Percent Bond
Maturing in 20 Years as a Function
of Prevailing Long-Term Interest Rates

Prevailing Long-Term Interest Rate	Bond Price
10%	$1,000
12	850
14	733
16	642
18	570
20	511

Conversion Value

The number of shares into which the debt instrument can be converted is established at the time of the underwriting. For illustration purposes assume that the hypothetical convertible under consideration is convertible into 40 shares of common stock; that is, the conversion ratio is 40. Exhibit 10–3 is a plot of the convertible price versus the stock price as determined by the conversion value. If the stock price is $10 the bond can be converted into 40 shares giving the convertible a value of $400. If the stock price is $20 the bond can be converted into stock and sold. Proceeds of the sale would be 40 shares times $20 or $800. Because the bond is convertible, the bond price follows the price of the underlying stock always remaining at or above the line defined as the conversion value.

The Convertible Track

Exhibit 10–4, the price boundaries, is a composite of Exhibit 10–1 and Exhibit 10–3. The bond will trade somewhere in the area above the solid lines. The bond will not trade below the

EXHIBIT 10-3
Conversion Value for a Hypothetical Convertible Bond

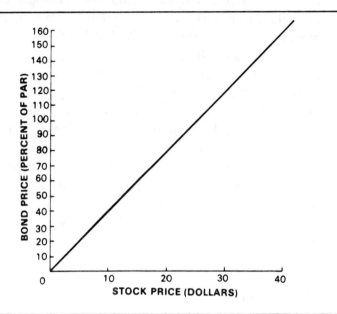

EXHIBIT 10-4
Boundary Conditions for a Hypothetical Convertible Bond

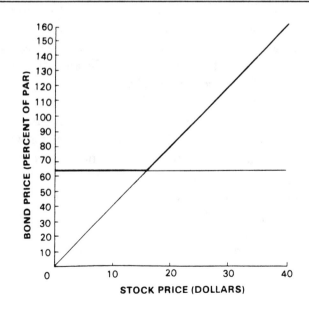

investment floor. If it did, astute buyers would enter the market until the yield returned to that for other instruments of similar quality. Similarly, the bond will not trade below conversion value. If it did, astute investors would buy the bonds, convert them, and sell the shares received for more than the cost of the bonds. Such activity assures that the bonds remain at conversion value as a minimum.

Exhibit 10–5 illustrates the typical price curve for a convertible bond, the hypothetical XYZ 10 percent bonds maturing in 20 years. The option feature provides the convertible with value over and above both the investment value and the conversion value. The amount by which the price exceeds the investment value or the conversion value is known as premium.

LATENT WARRANTS

This discussion has defined the convertible rather mechanically without reference to its option characteristics. However, by this time it should be clear that a convertible bond has many of the features of an option or a warrant, and Exhibit 10–5 clearly shows that a convertible bond is a straight bond with a warrant feature included. Because they cannot be detached from the bonds of which they are a part, these warrants are somewhat different from their freely traded counterparts. The warrant portion of a convertible is called a latent warrant to distinguish it from its cousins which trade without attachments. If the assumptions are made that the straight bond component can be priced accurately and that this value is recognized in the marketplace, then, given the inefficiencies in pricing warrants, an examination of the latent warrants may be rewarding.

Consider once again the hypothetical bonds discussed earlier—the XYZ 10 percent bonds maturing in 20 years. The price of the bond is $900. Each bond is convertible into

EXHIBIT 10–5
Convertible Price Curve

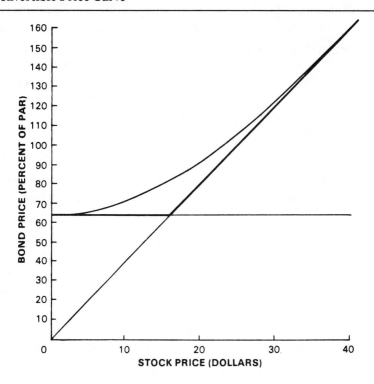

40 shares, and the investment value of the bond—that is, the value of similar quality bonds that are not convertible—is $650. Therefore the conversion feature is worth $250. The conversion privilege is equivalent to 40 latent warrants with a total worth of $250. Each latent warrant is therefore worth $250/40 or $6.25. Written symbolically, the price of the latent warrant is as follows:

$$W = \frac{C - I}{n} \qquad (10\text{--}1)$$

where W = price of latent warrant
     C = convertible price
     I = investment value
     n = conversion ratio

The exercise price of the warrants is the amount needed to convert them into common. Since the conversion consumes a bond worth $900, the exercise price per warrant is $900/40 or $22.50. Written symbolically, the exercise price for a latent warrant is as follows:

$$E = \frac{I}{n} \qquad (10\text{--}2)$$

where E = exercise price
     I = investment value
     n = conversion ratio

As with regular warrants these prices can be normalized and the values plotted on the warrant diagram. This is an excellent way of comparing the investment merits of various convertibles. It is also a means of identifying convertibles which may be ideally situated for hedging strategies. For the hypothetical bond under consideration, assume the stock price is 20 and the bond price is 90. Then S/E = 0.89 and W/E = 0.28. The normalized prices for the hypothetical XYZ convertible bond are plotted on the warrant diagram in Exhibit 10–6. The same techniques can also be used for evaluating convertible preferred stocks.

Latent Warrants versus Unattached Warrants

Latent warrants have three major shortcomings over their freely traded counterparts. The disadvantages generally cause the premiums for latent warrants to be lower. First, to acquire the latent warrant the bond must also be purchased, and ownership of the bonds introduces numerous investment complications. Second, the latent warrant does not have a definite expiration date since convertible bonds usually have a call feature which can cause retirement of the issue within a relatively short period. Third, the exercise price is not constant since it fluctuates with the investment worth of the convertible bond.

EXHIBIT 10–6
Selected Latent Warrants on the Warrant Diagram

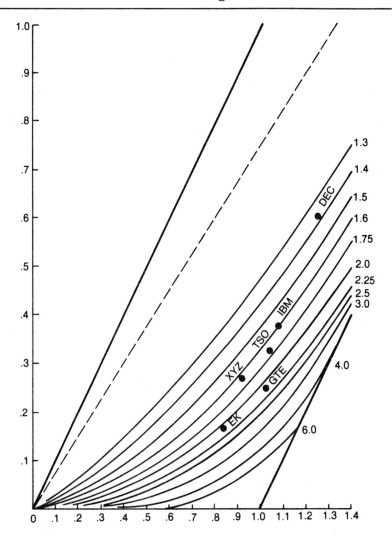

Selected Examples

The latent warrants for a few popular convertible bonds are calculated in Exhibit 10–7 and the results are plotted on the standard warrant diagram in Exhibit 10–6. These warrants

EXHIBIT 10-7
Latent Warrant Analysis for Selected Convertible Bonds

Company/Symbol	Digital Equipment (DEC)	Eastman Kodak (EK)	GTE Corp. (GTE)	International Business Machines (IBM)	Tesoro Petroleum (TSO)
Issue	8s 2009	8.25s 2007	10.5s 2007	7.875s 2004	5.25s 1989
Stock Yield*	Nil	5.5%	7.6%	3.6%	3.3%
Stock Volatility*	105%	60%	65%	65%	130%
Stock Price*	100.50	68.50	40.75	123.88	12.13
Convertible Price*	113.00	93.25	107.25	105.25	91.75
Conversion Ratio*	8.772	9.780	21.739	6.508	59.172
Investment Value*	71	79	86	76	69
Exercise Price $(E = I/n)$	80.940	80.777	39.560	116.779	11.661
Latent Warrant Price $[W = (C - I)/n]$	47.88	14.571	9.775	44.945	3.845
Normalized Stock Price (S/E)	1.24	.85	1.03	1.06	1.04
Normalized Warrant Price (W/E)	0.59	0.18	0.25	0.38	0.33

*Source: Value Line Convertibles, April 15, 1985.

have several characteristics in common: they are all long term, and the yield on the common is low. There is one significant difference: there is a wide range in the volatility of the underlying stock.

Tesoro Petroleum has the highest volatility of the issues under consideration; yet its track is not the highest. In fact, International Business Machines, with a low volatility, is on a much higher track. All other things being equal, the latent warrants for GTE Corporation, Eastman Kodak, and IBM should be on approximately the same track. This type of analysis will even turn up warrants which are more expensive than their unattached counterparts. Consider the Digital Equipment latent warrant. Given its location in the diagram it would not be a wise purchase as a traditional warrant.

This type of analysis indicates that other factors such as

sentiment may be extremely important in establishing convertible premiums. It may also be that ignorance prevails and that the proper worth is not understood. However, investors who believe that value is ultimately restored should restrict holdings to convertibles with cheap or fairly valued latent warrants.

SYNTHETIC CONVERTIBLES

Just as a convertible can be dissected into its component parts, a convertible can be synthesized when the appropriate building blocks are available. The only requirements are a warrant and a senior security which can be used at par value in lieu of cash when exercising the warrant.

Gluing together the component pieces is an attractive strategy when the warrant is on the bargain table. Even though its potential as an investment is superior, the risk inherent in the issue may still be too great for many investors. The addition of the bond tailors the risk, reducing the potential should the stock advance while moderating losses in the event of a stock decline.

The fabrication process is simple and easy to understand. For a conventional convertible, the straight bond portion is *surrendered* with the latent warrant portion to receive the number of shares equal to the bond's conversion ratio. In creating a synthetic convertible, warrants are purchased in conjunction with the usable bond. The number of warrants to purchase for each bond is determined by dividing the par value of the bond by the warrant's exercise price. The warrant-bond combination is then analyzed as a package. All of the parameters and figures of merit which can be computed for a conventional convertible can also be computed for the fabricated convertible.

Case Study: Nortek "Convertible Bonds"

To illustrate the fabrication process, securities for Nortek, Inc. have been chosen. Security statistics are shown in Exhibit 10–8, and the warrant value indicators are presented in Exhibit 10–9. From the evaluation matrix in Exhibit 6–14 we would expect the gamma factor to fall somewhere between 1.85 and 2.00. The actual value of 2.42 places the warrant very low in the diagram and indicates an undervalued situation.

The synthetic convertible is created by purchasing warrants in conjunction with the bonds. The number of warrants to accompany each bond is determined by dividing the par value of the bond by the warrant exercise price. For Nortek this number is 75 ($1,000/13.375). The complete investment strategy is as follows:

Buy 1M Nortek 15s2002 at 100 = $1,000
Buy 75 Nortek warrants at 4   =   300
Total Investment   = $1,300

At this point all the required information necessary to calculate various indicators of value for this synthetic convertible is available. These statistics are also included in Exhibit 10–8. The conversion value is the intrinsic value of the convertible and is obtained by multiplying the stock price times the conversion ratio ($75 \times \$16 = \$1,200$). The premium over conversion value is the difference between the bond price and the conversion value, expressed as a percentage of the conversion value. For the Nortek convertible this works out to a nominal 8.3 percent. The break-even time is defined as the time it would take for the convertible's premium over conversion value to be erased by the convertible's current yield advantage. For the Nortek convertible, this computes to 0.69 years (approximately 8 months).

Additional insight into the attractiveness of this synthetic convertible can be demonstrated through the leverage projections; that is, the performance of the convertible vis-à-vis the performance of the underlying common stock. These calculations are shown in Exhibit 10–10. In completing this table it was assumed that the bond price would remain constant as the stock price fluctuates. The price of the warrant for various levels of the stock price was calculated with the help of the

EXHIBIT 10–8
Security Statistics
Nortek, Inc.
Industry Group: Multiform
January 1985

Common Stock		Warrant	
Price	16	Price	4
Volatility	130%	Exercise price	13.375
Dividend	$.08	Conversion ratio	1.000
Yield	0.5%	Expiration	6-15-87
52-week high	$17\frac{3}{8}$	Time remaining	2.42 years
52-week low	12	Issue size	650,000
S&P rank	B +		

Usable Bond		Synthetic Convertible	
Issue	15s2002	Price	130
Price	100	Conversion ratio	75.00
Issue size	$26,000,000	Conversion value	$1200
Current yield	15%	Conversion premium	8.3%
Yield to maturity	15%	Break-even time	0.69 years
		Current yield	11.5%

EXHIBIT 10–9
Value Indicators
Nortek, Inc. Warrants
January 1985

Gamma Factor (γ)	2.419
Normalized Stock Price (S/E)	1.20
Normalized Warrant Price (W/E)	0.30
Premium (P1)	8.6
Premium (P2)	8.6
Leverage Indicator (LI)	4.0
Leverage Ratio (LR)	3.7
MathematicalAdvantage (MA)	2.2
Appreciation Multiple (M1)	4.7
Appreciation Multiple (M2)	1.1

EXHIBIT 10-10
Risk-Reward Analysis for the Nortek Synthetic Convertible

Stock Price Change	– 50%	– 25%	0%	+ 25%	+ 50%
Stock Price	8.00	12.00	16.00	20.00	24.00
Estimated Warrant Price	0.75	2.00	4.00	6.86	10.63
Bond Price	100	100	100	100	100
"Convertible" Price*	1056	1150	1300	1515	1797
Convertible Price Change	– 19%	– 12%	0%	+ 17%	+ 38%

*Equals the price of one bond plus 75 times the price of one latent warrant.

matrix in Exhibit 6–14. It was assumed that the gamma factor for the warrant (2.419) remained unchanged.

Attributes and Shortcomings

The identification of a grossly undervalued warrant usually means that a convertible with very attractive characteristics can be fabricated. Because the two components are not bonded together, the synthetic convertible has several advantages over its conventional counterpart. The ability to sell the individual components independently as prices change or as the investor's perception of the future changes is valuable. If the warrant returns to its normal value, there will be an opportunity to nail down profits. Depending upon the outlook for the stock market and interest rates, one or both of the synthetic convertible components may be sold to capitalize on that outlook.

Pitfalls develop if the warrant is not selected with care. All the terms must be known in advance. Special features such as step-ups in the exercise price or call provisions will sabotage the investor's position. Finally, if the warrant is in-the-money, it usually would be wise to sell the bond prior to the warrant's expiration, since the loss of the bond's usability feature could cause its value to drop.

CHAPTER

11

SPECIAL CONSIDERATIONS

INTRODUCTION

There are a number of loose ends with respect to warrant trading which could not be covered conveniently in the preceding chapters. Although described here as miscellaneous and appearing late in the book, their importance should not be underestimated. These items are not only essential to a warrant trader's knowledge but they also have some fascinating elements as well. The purpose of this chapter is to bring these final items to the investor's attention and to wrap up the warrant story.

MORE ON USABLE BONDS

As noted earlier, warrants frequently originate as part of a package combined with straight (non-convertible) debt. In such combinations there frequently is a provision that the bond can be used at par value in lieu of cash if the warrant is exercised. Thus, when exercising, the warrant holder has a choice: to submit cash or to surrender the usable bond. If the bond is selling at par or higher, the usability feature provides no advantage to the warrant holder. However, if the bond is selling below par it effectively offers a discount in the exercise price.

While certainly attractive to the owner, this provision may be attractive to the issuer as well. This privilege makes it possible for the company to retire its debt without cash payment since debentures used to exercise warrants are canceled.

YIELD TO EARLY MATURITY

An interesting investment opportunity often develops in long term usable bonds which are likely to be surrendered during warrant exercise. Such bonds are priced similarly to other bonds having similar quality and duration. However, if the warrant is in the money, exercise is certain. The discounted bonds will therefore be purchased to capitalize on the reduced exercise price. This unusual demand will influence the bond price, and it will be driven to par or thereabouts effectively shortening its maturity to the expiration date of the warrant. Thus the *yield to early maturity* may be significantly higher than the conventional yield to maturity.

The conditions necessary for a bond to be profitable under such conditions are as follows:

1.   The usable bond is selling below par,
2.   The warrant will expire in-the-money,
3.   The warrant expiration date is much sooner than the bond maturity date, and

4.   The exercise must consume the entire bond issue.

The rationale for each of these conditions is as follows. If the warrant is in-the-money it will be exercised. If the usable bond is below par it will be purchased to capitalize on the lower effective exercise price. Since the supply of bonds is less than or equal to the amount needed to exercise the complete warrant issue, all the existing bonds will be demanded by warrant owners until such time as the bond price approaches par.

Exhibit 11–1 provides relevant data for the usable bonds available as of December 1984. It contains all the information necessary to analyze the impact and effects of usable bonds. In the table, yield to maturity is calculated in the conventional way. Yield to early maturity is calculated assuming that the bond "matures" (approaches par) at the warrant expiration date.

The column labeled *outstanding debt* is the issue size of the usable bond. The *debt required for exercise* is obtained by multiplying the number of outstanding warrants by the warrant exercise price. The *availability factor* is the principal amount of the bonds necessary for complete warrant exercise (using bonds exclusively) expressed as a percentage.

The yield to maturity has been calculated for every usable bond. In reality, only those bonds having an availability factor less than or equal to 100 percent will have prices influenced by the exercise procedure. If the number of bonds is substantially larger than the number needed to exercise the complete warrant issue, the preceding strategy will not work. Since there is not potential demand for all the bonds the market will supply those needed to warrant holders at a price which maintains the bond's yield to maturity close to that which would prevail if the warrant perturbation did not exist.

For usable bonds likely to be submitted in the exercise process, the "exercise effect" will probably be anticipated thus causing the yield to maturity for usable bonds to be less

EXHIBIT 11-1
Bonds Usable to Exercise Warrants in Lieu of Cash*

Corporation/ Warrant	Stock Price	Warrants Out- standing (millions)	Warrant Exercise Price	Warrant Expiration Date	Bond Coupon/ Maturity	Bond Price	Bond Grade (S&P)	Yield to Maturity (%)	Yield to Early Maturity (%)	Debt Avail- able (millions)	Debt Required for Exercise (millions)	Avail- ability Factor (%)
Beker Indus- tries 1988 wt	5.50	2.340	10.00	7/1/88	15 7/8-03 7/1/03	97 1/2	CCC	16.31	16.81	65.0	23.4	278
Caesars World 1985 wt	10.00	.920	24.50	8/1/85	12 1/2-00 8/15/00	94 1/4	B NR	13.34	22.80	2.70	22.5	12
Cannon Group 1989 wt	18.63	2.100	25.00	11/1/89	12 3/8-94 11/1/94	86	NR	15.15	16.69	70.0	52.5	133
Charter Co	1.13	3.357	10.00	9/1/88	10 5/8-98 9/1/98	22 1/4	D	Bond in Default	N/A	46.1	33.6	137
Digicon Inc	2.25	.945	16.50	6/15/88	12 7/8-93 6/15/93	80 1/2	CCC	17.67	21.08	35.0	15.6	224
Electronic Memories & Magnetics 1988 wt	4.75	1.453	12.00	6/1/88	10.7-93 6/1/93	77	B-	15.71	20.33	17.5	17.4	100
FMI Financial 1988 wt	5.25	7.260	11.38	4/29/88	9-93 5/1/93	75	CCC	14.20	19.53	82.5	82.6	100
FPA Corp. 1988 wt	9.38	1.500	12.00	8/15/88	12 5/8-93 8/15/93	65	B+	21.76	28.73	30.0	18.0	167
Frontier Holdings (Air)	14.00	.462	9.15	3/1/87	5 1/2-87 3/1/87	81	B-	16.20	16.20	5.28	4.2	125

Fuqua Industries 1988 wt	30.38	.602	30.78	6/30/88	7-88 7/1/88	$93\frac{1}{2}$	B	9.21	9.21	10.8	18.5	58
Genesco Oct 15 1993 wt	5.50	.900	11.75	10/15/93	$9\frac{3}{4}$-93 10/15/93	75	B–	14.94	14.94	30.0	10.6	284
Geothermal Resources	8.25	.600	13.50	11/15/91	13-91 11/15/91	$86\frac{1}{4}$	NR	16.39	16.39	15.0	8.1	185
Golden Nugget 1988 wt	9.38	15.000	18.00	7/1/88	$8\frac{3}{8}$-93 7/1/93	$69\frac{3}{4}$	B+	14.72	25.39	250	270	93
Grolier Inc 1988 wt	3.00	2.050	6.00	11/1/88	$13\frac{5}{8}$-03 11/1/03	$83\frac{5}{8}$	B	16.45	16.45	82.0	12.3	667
HPSC Inc 1989 wt	5.75	2.500	11.00	1/15/89	10-94 11/15/94	$74\frac{1}{2}$	NR	15.29	19.36	20.0	27.5	73
International Banknote	3.50	5.720	7.00	7/31/88	10-98 4/1/98	62	NR	17.42	27.21	40.0	40.0	100
International Harvester	8.00	10.845	5.00	12/15/93	18-02 12/15/02	$106\frac{1}{2}$	CCC	16.84	16.58	65.1	54.2	120
MCI Communications	7.50	36.000	27.50	8/1/88	$9\frac{1}{2}$-93 8/1/93	76	BB	14.46	19.00	1000	990	101
M.D.C. Corp 1988 wt	11.50	3.080	18.00	4/15/88	7-93 4/15/93	75	B+	11.80	17.24	55.0	55.4	99
MGM/UA Entertainment	11.88	2.515	20.0	4/14/88	10-93 4/15/93	$79\frac{1}{4}$	BB–	15.17	18.70	400.0	50.3	795
McDermott International	24.38	5.999	25.00	4/1/90	10-03 4/1/03	$82\frac{1}{8}$	A–	12.50	15.02	150.0	150.0	100
McLean Industries 1990 wt	11.13	8.998	11.20	7/15/90	12-03 7/15/03	81	B–	15.07	17.48	118.0	100.8	117

EXHIBIT 11-1 Continued
Bonds Usable to Exercise Warrants in Lieu of Cash*

Corporation/ Warrant	Stock Price	Warrants Out-standing (millions)	Warrant Exercise Price	Warrant Expiration Date	Bond Coupon/ Maturity	Bond Price	Bond Grade (S&P)	Yield to Maturity (%)	Yield to Early Maturity (%)	Debt Avail-able (millions)	Debt Required for Exercise (millions)	Avail-ability Factor (%)
Minstar Inc 1989 wt	18.50	4.400	14.50	2/1/89	12½-96 2/1/96	90	NR	14.32	15.90	100.0	63.8	157
NCNB Corp 1992 wt	35.75	.170	18.18	8/1/92	7¾-02 8/1/02	65	A	12.79	15.82	50.0	3.1	1618
Nortek Inc	15.00	.650	13.38	6/15/87	15-02 6/15/02	100	B	15.00	N/A	26.0	8.7	299
Occidental Petroleum	27.75	7.700	25.00	4/14/87	8.95-94 4/15/94	84	BBB-	11.83	17.71	700	192.5	364
Orion Pictures 1989 wt	8.50	2.100	20.50	2/1/89	10-94 2/1/94	73¼	B	15.59	19.83	50.0	43.1	116
Pan Am Corp	4.50	10.000	8.00	5/1/93	13½-03 5/1/03	76	B-	18.00	19.40	100.0	80.0	125
Penril Corp 1988 wt	12.00	1.260	14.00	2/1/88	10⅞-93 2/1/93	81	B-	15.00	19.29	18.0	17.6	102
Petro-Lewis 1988 wt	4.00	6.358	16.61	2/15/88	11¼-93 2/15/93	71	B	18.53	25.45	85.0	105.6	80
Public Service New Hampshire	3.88	11.119	5.00	10/15/91	17½-04 10/15/04	84	CCC	20.89	22.13	130.0	55.6	234

Company												
Storer Communications	46.00	2.300	40.00	5/13/88	10-03 5/15/03	75	BB−	13.76	20.62	230.0	92.0	250
Tele-Communications	23.25	5.750	21.70	1/1/88	$11\frac{1}{2}$-95 1/1/95	88	B+	15.50	16.73	125.0	124.8	100
Texas International 1988 wt	1.25	.900	8.91	7/14/88	$13\frac{3}{8}$-93 7/15/93	52	CCC	28.26	39.31	100.0	8.0	1247
Tiger International 1988 wt	6.25	3.213	12.50	6/30/88	$8\frac{5}{8}$-95 10/1/95	52	NR	19.39	32.57	14.5	40.2	36
Triangle Industries 1993 wt	16.75	.258	18.50	9/1/93	$11\frac{1}{2}$-03 9/1/03	77	B−	15.24	16.58	90.0	4.8	1886
Tyler Corp	29.50	3.000	34.00	11/1/87	$12\frac{7}{8}$-94 11/1/94	94	BB+	14.01	15.54	100.0	102.0	98
Unifi Inc.	8.13	.900	11.28	7/1/88	$12\frac{1}{4}$-88 7/1/88	101	B	11.89	11.89	20.0	10.2	197
USAir Group Inc 1987 "O" wt	34.25	.414	17.31	4/1/87	$5\frac{1}{2}$-87 4/1/87	$85\frac{1}{2}$	BBB	13.11	13.11	10.0	7.2	140
U.S. Playing Card	14.50	1.830	16.38	6/15/90	$9\frac{7}{8}$-93 12/15/93	$72\frac{1}{4}$	NR	15.76	18.07	30.0	30.0	100
Webb, Del E Corp	20.50	.575	26.00	4/15/88	$11\frac{1}{2}$-88 4/15/88	99	B	11.86	11.86	28.8	15.0	193
Western Air Lines 1993 wt	3.50	9.000	9.50	6/15/93	$10\frac{3}{4}$-98 6/15/98	$63\frac{7}{8}$	B−	17.94	19.68	90.0	85.5	105

*Statistics as of December 28, 1984

than the yield to maturity for equivalent bonds with no warrant connection. Risk is therefore incurred—in particular, risk that the stock price will decline and the warrant will be out-of-the-money at expiration and therefore not exercised. The artificial demand for the bonds created by warrant holders will evaporate, and the bond price will drop until its yield to maturity matches that of equivalent issues.

Case Study: McDermott International 10s of 2003

This debenture is a high quality (S&P rank is A-) security with a yield to maturity (12.54%) in line with other securities of similar quality and duration. It was originally issued as a unit with stock purchase warrants. Current statistics for the McDermott securities are given in Exhibit 11-2.

The bond is usable at par value in lieu of cash when exercising the warrants, a feature which gives the bond considerably greater value than is currently acknowledged in the marketplace. The warrant exercise price is $25 but by using the bond the effective exercise price is reduced to $20.50 (82 percent of $25). Thus, with the stock at current levels, the warrants will be exercised and bonds will be purchased for this purpose. This artificial demand will force the bond to par by the warrant's expiration date (April 1, 1990). The yield to maturity for the bonds calculated in the normal way is 12.54 percent. This yield is appropriate for a bond of this quality and duration. Should the warrants be exercised in 1990, the yield to early maturity is 15.21 percent, 267 basis points higher. To obtain such a yield elsewhere would require bonds of considerably lower quality—in particular, those having an S&P grade of B-.

There are two additional special provisions for the warrant which further influence this situation:

1. The company can accelerate the expiration date to April 1, 1988 if the common is at least 125 percent of the

EXHIBIT 11-2
Security Statistics
McDermott International
Industry Group: Oilfield Services
March 1985

Common Stock		Debenture	
Price	$27\frac{1}{2}$	Issue	10s of 2002
Volatility	110%	Price	82
Dividend	$1.80	Issue size	$150,000,000
52-week high	$31\frac{5}{8}$	S&P rank	A −
52-week low	$23\frac{1}{2}$	Current yield	12.20%
S&P rank	B	Yield to maturity	12.54%

Warrant	
Price	$8\frac{1}{4}$
Exercise price	$25.00
Effective exercise price	$20.50
Conversion ratio	1.000
Expiration	4-01-90
Issue size	5,999,000

exercise price for 20 days within a 30 consecutive trading day period, and

2. The company has the right to reduce the exercise price by one third at any time.

The purpose of these features is to permit the issuer to force exercise of the warrants. Thus debt is converted to equity giving the issuer partial control over the company's capitalization.

The first provision becomes effective when the common is above 31 1/4, and the second provision is in effect currently. Both of these provisions will encourage exercise of the warrants earlier than the stated expiration date. Acceleration of the expiration date will enhance the yield to early maturity even further. However, reduction of the exercise price will probably not influence the bond price. With the exercise price at $25 the entire bond issue is consumed if the warrant is exercised. With a lower exercise price only a portion of the bond issue is retired. Thus the supply of bonds will be more than sufficient to meet demands from warrant holders intending to exercise.

SHORT SALES

To effect a short sale, securities are borrowed and sold on the open market. Collateral in the form of margin must be posted as protection for the lender. If the shares subsequently decline in price, they are repurchased and returned to the lender. The profit—as is the case with any transaction—is the difference between the purchase price and the sale price. However, when selling short, the order of the transactions is reversed. If the securities rise in price instead of fall, they are repurchased at a higher level. Since the purchase price is higher than the sale price a loss results.

When selling short several obstacles may be encountered. First, the shares may be difficult to borrow. Second, the margin requirements may be unfavorable. Third, the brokerage house through which the transaction is directed may have special restrictions regarding short sales. Fourth, it may not be possible to retain the short position as long as desired. Finally, the exchange may have prohibited short sales in the issue of interest. The following is a detailed discussion of each of these obstacles:

1. The shares to be sold short must be borrowed from someone. Margin investors must sign an agreement with their brokerage firm which includes a provision allowing the house to lend the purchased shares to another investor for

short selling. If the size of the issue is small, locating the shares to borrow may be difficult. Because of the margin agreement, shorting marginable issues is much easier than shorting non-marginable issues. However, any security can be sold short. The brokerage house may lend shares that it holds in its own account or shares owned by another client (if permission can be obtained to do so) even if the securities are not marginable. If the securities are not available in-house, they can be borrowed from another brokerage firm that has an available supply.

2. As will be discussed in the following section, special margin requirements apply when selling short low priced issues. This margin may be in excess of 100 percent of the value of the shares shorted. When incorporating such issues into a strategy the investor must calculate the profit profile taking into account the total equity in the portfolio. An investor using margin only to a limited degree may find low priced warrants attractive in certain positions regardless of the margin requirement.

3. Some brokerage houses limit short sales to securities which are marginable. In addition they may impose stricter margin requirements than those established by the Federal Reserve and the various exchanges.

4. When the total number of shares sold short (a statistic called the short interest) is large the possibility exists that the lender will request return of the borrowed shares and that other shares cannot be located as a replacement. At that point the shares must be covered by the investor, and, if this action is not taken promptly, the brokerage firm will execute the purchase transaction, a procedure known as a buy-in. It is therefore possible that a position with substantial profit potential remaining will be terminated prematurely.

5. When the short interest in a listed security gets too high, the exchange gets concerned about the possibility of a short squeeze. At that point they may restrict further shorting of

that issue. A short squeeze is a condition in which sellers are scarce and panic buying by those with short positions causes large price excursions.

The above list may seem formidable. However large portfolios with diversified warrant positions can be maintained if caution is exercised and the investor researches each position thoroughly in advance.

MARGIN REQUIREMENTS

The rules for setting warrant margins are complicated. While the rule for a long position is a simple percentage, the rules for short positions vary depending upon the price of the issue and the securities it accompanies. Certain hedged positions require even further complications of the rules.

The basic rules for unhedged positions are shown in Exhibit 11–3. Figure 1 shows graphically the margin requirement for warrant long positions. The current margin requirement is 50 percent, independent of the price of the underlying stock. Figure 2 shows graphically the margin requirement for warrant short positions. When the stock price is at $2.50 or lower, the margin required is a constant $2.50. Thus, for low priced issues the margin requirement can be several hundred percent. For a stock price between $2.50 and $5.00 the margin requirement is 100 percent. For a stock price between $5 and $10 the margin requirement is constant at $5. At $10 and above the requirement is 50 percent, just as it is for long positions.

Margin requirements for various hedges using both warrant long positions and warrant short positions are shown in Exhibit 11–4. Generally speaking, the margin for a hedge is the sum of the margin required for the individual components of the hedge. Case 4 is an interesting exception. When convertibles (including warrants) are held long in an account—even if purchased on margin—no margin is required for an accompanying short position in the securities for which

EXHIBIT 11-3
Margin Requirements
Warrant Long and Short Positions

FIGURE 1

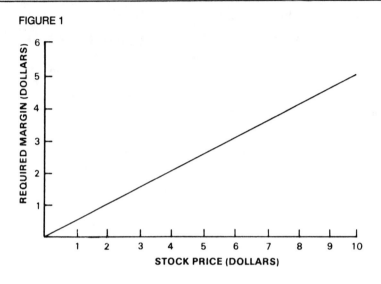

FIGURE 2

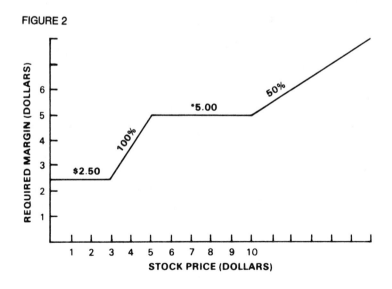

EXHIBIT 11–4
Margin Requirements
Warrant Hedge Positions

Transaction	Minimum Initial Margin		Notes
Long Stock & Short Warrant	Stock: Warrant:	50% 50%*	1. Margin computed separately for each position. Hedge margin is sum of components.
Long Convertible Preferred & Short Warrant	Convertible: Warrant:	50% 50%*	2. Same as Note 1.
Long Convertible Bond & Short Warrant	Convertible: Warrant:	50% 50%*	3. Same as Note 1.
Long Warrant & Short Stock	Warrant: Stock:	50% 0	4. Special provisions of Regulation T, Section 220.3(d)(3) apply.
Long Warrant & Short Call Option	Hedge $\begin{cases} \text{Warrant:} & 50\% \\ \text{plus} \\ E_{Long} - E_{Short} \\ \text{less} \\ \text{option premium} \\ \text{received} \end{cases}$		5. E_{Long} is the warrant exercise price and E_{Short} is the option exercise price.
Long Call Option & Short Warrant	Call: Warrant:	100% 50%*	6. Same as Note 1.

*Subject to special minimums for low priced issues.

the convertible can be exchanged. This requirement is a provision of the Federal Reserve System Regulation T, Section 220.3(d)(3) pertaining to margin requirements which reads in part:

. . . such amount as the Board shall prescribe from time to time . . . as the margin required for short sales, except that such amount so prescribed . . . need not be included when there are held in the account securities exchangeable or convertible within 90 calendar days, without restriction other than the payment of money, into such securities sold short . . .

An example of an application of this rule was given in Chapter 8 involving hedging of Warner Communications securities—specifically, the purchase of WCI warrants and the short sale of WCI common.

COMMISSIONS

Commissions charged for warrant transactions are calculated in exactly the same way as commissions for stock transactions. As most investors are now aware, there is no consistency among brokerage firms, and the range between the cheapest and the most expensive is quite large. Unfortunately, it is difficult to do business at the cheapest discounter because the broker must provide some assistance in executing the transactions, especially when hedging is being attempted.

A good broker gets good executions which will more than pay for the higher transaction costs. However, even firms with seemingly rigid commission structures are open to negotiation, especially if orders are large and the account is active. The broker may also be the source of additional ideas. Because they are so close to the markets they may discover interesting price relationships on a more timely basis. They may also have other clients involved in similar strategies and once the client is fully invested these ideas can generally be passed along.

TAXES

With respect to long term and short term gains, warrants are taxed like common stocks (as of June 1984 the crossover point is six months). The tax consequences for warrant holders who elect to exercise can be very unfavorable and a real eye-opener for unknowledgeable investors. When warrants are exercised the basis of the securities acquired equals the cost of the warrants plus the cash required for exercise. The holding period for the securities acquired begins on the day after the warrants are exercised. Once again the rule that warrants are purchased to be sold, not exercised, seems to be justified.

CHAPTER
12

AMERICUS TRUSTS: UNITS, PRIMES AND SCORES

INTRODUCTION

One of the goals of developers of new financial products has been the creation of an equity alternative incorporating a way to separate future income and growth. Albeit limited, efforts have met with success through two vehicles—dual-purpose funds and Americus Trusts.

The dual-purpose funds accomplish the goal with closed-end mutual funds. Initially, two types of shares are created—income shares and capital shares. Holders of the income shares are entitled to all the dividends which the investments produce. Holders of the capital shares receive all the capital gains which the investments produce.

A pure equity product came in 1983 with the introduction of the Americus Trusts. The concept is basically simple.

The trust acts as a repository for common shares which are exchanged for a certificate divisible into two parts: one part entitles the holder to all the income and some modest appreciation from the underlying shares while the other part entitles the holder to all the appreciation in price of the underlying common above a preset dollar amount.

The Americus Trust was originally available only for shares of the pre-divestiture AT&T. Recently, however, the basic concept has been approved for other stocks and the offerings have been initiated.

The separation of a stock's income and growth components has broad implications for a wide variety of investors. However, because of the similarity to a stock purchase warrant, it is the growth component which is of primary interest in this discussion.

BASIC CONCEPTS

Special rulings by the Internal Revenue Service and the Securities and Exchange Commission permit Americus Shareowner Service Corporation to sponsor trusts in selected stock issues. When an investor trades in a share of one of the eligible issues it is exchanged for an Americus Trust Unit. Once the Unit is obtained, the investor can concentrate on either the income or growth alternative.

Unit Characteristics

Each Unit can be separated into two parts, the PRIME™ component and the SCORE™ component. Once detached, the components can be marketed individually. The PRIME component entitles the holder to the income on the underlying stock while the SCORE component entitles the holder to the growth in the underlying stock.

™Trademarks of Americus Shareholder Service Corporation representing the components of the Bi-Partite Stock Certificate covered by Patent No. 4,093,276 dated June 6, 1978.

All Americus Trusts have a life of five years. At any time during the life of the trust, original Units can be redeemed for an amount equal to net asset value. Similarly, Units created by the recombination of the PRIME and SCORE components can be redeemed at net asset value. The recombination and redemption features were designed to prevent the trading price of the Units and the combined trading price of the PRIME and SCORE components from falling below the value of the underlying shares.

PRIME Characteristics

The component which entitles the holder to the income is called a PRIME (Prescribed Right to Income and Maximum Equity). It carries rights to dividends from the underlying stock, voting rights, and stock price appreciation up to a predetermined ceiling called the *Termination Claim.* Except for the cap on the appreciation in value that can accrue to a PRIME, it is very similar to a regular share of stock. PRIME component holders get almost the same dividends they would get if they owned the actual stock—but at a discount from the stock's market price. The discount is equal to the value of the SCORE component. The PRIME component is more stable than the stock and best suited for income oriented investors.

SCORE Characteristics

The component which entitles the holder to the equity's growth is called a SCORE (Special Claim On Residual Equity). It entitles the holder to any appreciation above the termination ceiling. SCOREs are similar to long term call options or warrants and the Termination Claim is equivalent to the strike price or the exercise price. The SCORE component is more volatile and risky than either the common stock or the PRIME component.

Setting the Termination Claim

Establishing the Termination Claim involves consideration of several factors. The favorable tax ruling under which the trust operates covers only those deposits made when the stock is below the Termination Claim. Therefore the Termination Claim must be set high enough initially to provide a cushion against a rapid advance in the stock price before the trust offering is completed. Once the minimum cushion has been determined, the Termination Claim may be further adjusted to optimize both the potential yield to maturity for the PRIME buyer and the leverage for the SCORE buyer.

SCORE SHARES AS WARRANTS

In the preceding section the similarity between warrants and the SCOREs was addressed. A more thorough comparison—one which includes call options—is given in Exhibit 12–1. From the perspectives established in this book, both in terms of speculating and hedging, SCOREs possess distinct advantages over their warrant counterparts and these are provided without the introduction of negative factors.

SCORE Attributes

Any listing of SCORE attributes would necessarily include the following:

1. All of the forthcoming Americus Trust issues are potentially very large, ranging in size from 3,500,000 shares to 10,000,000 shares. Thus, the liquidity should be excellent.
2. All the new issues will be listed on the American Stock Exchange and all will be marginable. Data such as

EXHIBIT 12-1
Distinguishing Characteristics of Scores, Warrants and Call Options

	Scores	Warrants	Exchange-Traded Options
1. Origination or creation	From a trust Unit separable into a PRIME & SCORE component and backed by underlying stock.	Principally issued by corporations.	May be sold naked or from fully covered stock position.
2. Secondary market	AMEX listed trading.	AMEX, NYSE or OTC	On option exchanges.
3. Marginable	Yes	Yes	No
4. Equity security	Yes	No	No
5. Potential for dilution	No	Yes	No
6. Potential for long-term capital gain	Yes	Yes	Yes
7. Intrinsic value	Almost always	Depends on relationship of stock price to exercise price.	Depends on relationship of stock price to exercise price.
8. Exerciseable before maturity	Only together with a PRIME	Yes with cash	Yes with cash
9. Liability accounting by writer (seller)	None	None	Always
10. Loss of value if unexercised	No	Yes	No
11. Method of exercise and settlement at maturity	SCORE exchanged for stock	Warrant plus cash for stock	Exercise notice plus cash for stock
12. Special tax considerations	Yes if PRIME is retained	No	No

Source: Americus Shareowner Service Corporation

prices and the short interest will be easy to obtain.
3. The SCORE terms are fixed. The nuisance factors associated with existing warrants such as accelerations or extensions of the expiration date, increases or decreases of the exercise price, call provisions and the like are not associated with SCOREs.
4. The underlying stocks are for highly visible companies. It will be easy to keep abreast of developments within these companies and statistical data will be readily available.

SCORE Negatives

Only one potential negative surfaces and that is the question of liquidity. At this particular juncture it is not possible to determine the ultimate acceptance of the PRIMEs and SCOREs. The proposed offerings are large and the time constraints are such that this relatively ambitious undertaking may not be fully realized. If liquidity never develops, most of the potentially interesting things which can be done with warrants will be disallowed—prevented by large bid/ asked spreads, poor market depth, and the inability to borrow shares for shorting.

AMERICUS TRUSTS VERSUS DUAL-PURPOSE FUNDS

Americus Trusts are frequently compared with dual-purpose funds. It is worthwhile to explore the similarities and differences between these two types of investments, especially in view of the fact that both are having a resurgence of popularity.

The dual-purpose funds are publicly-traded (closed-end) mutual funds. At the offering two types of securities—both having equal value—are issued, the income shares and the capital shares. Holders of the income shares receive all the interest and dividends on the underlying portfolio while holders of the capital shares receive all the gains or losses. For each $1 put into the fund, $2 is working towards the investor's particular goal.

All the dual-purpose funds have a fixed life and at the termination date they are liquidated. The income shareholders receive a fixed redemption price plus dividend arrearages. The capital shareholders receive the remaining assets of the fund. Neither class of shares can be redeemed before the termination date but active trading markets exist and purchase or sale of the shares is easily accomplished.

In contrast to the Americus Trusts, the dual-purpose funds represent portfolios, not individual issues. There is a tendency for the capital shares to trade at a discount from net asset value, a consequence of the fact that the issues are not redeemable until the termination date of the trust. Dual-purpose funds received enthusiastic support in the late 1960s but the concept failed to retain investor interest and all but one of the funds (Hemisphere) have matured. Recently, however, new dual-purpose funds have been introduced with construction and objectives similar to those of the original funds.

HISTORY

The Americus Trust concept was developed in the early 1970s by A. Joseph Debe. He originated the concept and through dedication and perseverance overcame the bureaucratic and legislative roadblocks which prevented implementation of his idea. Mr. Debe is currently president of Americus Shareowner Service Corp., the sponsor of the trusts.

Implementation of the Americus Trusts has been hindered through several different avenues. The regulatory authorities—namely the Internal Revenue Service and the Securities and Exchange Commission—reviewed and ruled on the trusts. Some of the underlying companies are opposed to the concept and they made known their concerns to the regulators, the exchanges, and the underwriters. The New York Stock Exchange, coping with unique pressures, refused to list the new Americus Trusts. Finally, some underwriters found more negatives than positives in being involved with the offerings and therefore changes were necessary in this arena.

Technicalities of the various issues which concerned the IRS and the SEC are complex and not relevant to this text. Suffice it to say that it was a major undertaking to get approval from each of these agencies and both required several submissions of the trust proposal before the final go-ahead was granted.

Although the NYSE listed the original Americus Trust for AT&T, that exchange subsequently instituted a moratorium on all unit investment trusts and therefore refused to list any additional Americus Trust offerings. Concern was expressed about the unknowns surrounding these issues. Specifically it was stated that a proliferation of trusts could lead to investor confusion and, because SCORE holders cannot vote and do not receive corporate information, disrupt a corporation's communications with stockholders. It is possible also that the NYSE moratorium was a result of pressure placed on the exchange by certain of the large corporations scheduled for trust offerings. Nearly half of the companies were opposed to the concept and all of the companies are NYSE listed.

None of the corporations whose shares were being placed in Americus Trusts was ecstatic about the concept. In fact, their position ranged from lethargic to adamantly opposed. The most active opponent was John Rotenstreich, corporate treasurer of IBM. His primary argument is that Americus creates two classes of shareholders with competing interests. One class benefits from current earnings and dividends and the other from long term growth. Many unknowns exist and the companys involved do have the legitimate right to be cautious in endorsing a new concept such as the Americus Trust. Of course, equally valid concerns surfaced when listed options debuted on the Chicago Board Option Exchange. At that time no one knew the possible influences of one security on the other and challenging questions about manipulation and price distortion were raised. Nevertheless, a peaceful coexistence, acceptable to most of the entities involved, has emerged.

Even underwriters have been required to position themselves to protect their interests in view of the attitude of large current or potential clients. The first Americus Trust, that for AT&T, was marketed by a group led by Kidder, Peabody & Company and included E. F. Hutton & Company, Smith Barney, Harris Upham & Company, A. G. Edwards & Sons, and Thomson McKinnon Securities. Although the Americus prospectus provided for the exchange of up to 45 million shares, only slightly more than 6 million shares were tendered. Citing the time and effort associated with the educational process which must accompany the deal, Kidder Peabody has declined to be involved in subsequent offerings. Once again, keeping in good graces with large potential corporate clients may have motivated this decision. For the current series the dealer-managers are Furman Selz Mager Dietz & Birney, Inc. and Alex. Brown & Sons.

THE AMERICUS TRUST UNIVERSE

Although the Americus Trust concept has been in development for more than seven years, only two tangible exchanges have materialized thus far. The first occurred in October 1983 and was for pre-divestiture AT&T shares. The second occurred in September 1985 for Exxon shares. The most recent offering is only the first of many more that are scheduled.

Future Listings

Companies targeted for new Americus Trusts are listed in Exhibit 12–2. In addition to the Americus Trust for Exxon, trusts for another 29 stocks are planned. The undertaking is ambitious, especially in view of the fact that it must occur within a two year period. If completely successful, 243,500,000 new SCOREs (warrants) will debut.

Americus Trust for AT&T Common Shares, Series A

The first Americus Trust was introduced in October 1983. Units were exchanged for pre-divestiture AT&T common stock placed in the trust. The Americus Trust for AT&T attracted only moderate investor interest. The original offer was to exchange up to 45 million Units for AT&T shares tendered. Expectations were overly optimistic as only slightly more than six million shares were tendered. The termination date is October 24, 1988 and the Termination Claim is $75. The Units (ticker symbol TUA) as well as the PRIME (TPA) and SCORE (TSA) components trade on the New York Stock Exchange. In late October 1985 the Units were priced at 79 5/8, the PRIMEs at 67 3/4, and the SCOREs at 12 3/8.

After the breakup each Unit became the equivalent of one new AT&T share plus one-tenth of a share of each of the seven new regional companies. Thus, the SCORE component is now a warrant on a package of low volatility utility-type securities.

The Americus Trust for AT&T has provided an interesting test case regarding the relative pricing of Units, PRIMEs and SCOREs. Some analysts believed there would be great similarity between Americus securities and the dual-pur-

EXHIBIT 12-2
The Americus Stocks

Company Name	Symbol	Units Offered
American Express	AXP	7,500,000
American Home Products	AHP	7,500,000
Amoco Corporation	AN	10,000,000
American Telephone & Telegraph (new)	T	10,000,000
Atlantic Richfield	ARC	10,000,000
Bristol-Myers	BMY	5,000,000
Chevron Corporation	CHV	10,000,000
Coca-Cola Company	KO	5,000,000
Dow Chemical Company	DOW	7,500,000
Du Pont Compnay	DD	10,000,000
Eastman Kodak	EK	7,500,000
Exxon Corporation	XON	10,000,000
Ford Motor Company	F	9,000,000
GTE Corporation	GTE	7,500.000
General Electric Company	GE	10,000,000
General Motors Corporation	GM	10,000,000
Hewlett-Packard	HWP	10,000,000
International Business Machines	IBM	10,000,000
Johnson & Johnson	JNJ	7,500,000
Merck & Company	MRK	3,500,000
Minnesota Mining & Manufacturing	MMM	5,000,000
Mobil Corporation	MOB	10,000,000
Philip Morris	MO	5,000,000
Proctor & Gamble	PG	7,500,000
Royal Dutch Petroleum	RD	10,000,000
Schlumberger Ltd.	SLB	10,000,000
Sears, Roebuck & Company	S	10,000,000
Texaco Inc.	TX	10,000,000
Union Pacific	UNP	5,000,000
Xerox Corporation	XRX	3,500,000

pose funds. For the latter, the price of the two components fell below the fund's net asset value after the initial offering.

However, the dual-purpose funds cannot be redeemed until the trust is terminated (the typical fund matures in a decade). The Americus Trust should not behave similarly since the PRIME and SCORE components can be combined and turned in to receive the underlying stock at any time without a fee. Theoretically, at least, the continuous redemption feature should guarantee that the components will, at a minimum, always add up to the value of the underlying stock.

In fact, Units of the AT&T trust have traded below the value of the old AT&T stock at times. Given its touted flexibility, the Unit should always have a built-in premium according to some analysts. The discount may be attributed to the fact that the vehicles are new and not well understood. Americus points out that the issue never traded at a discount before February 15, 1984, the date when the break-up was finalized and before the stock price of what is now the old AT&T become difficult to ascertain, thereby eliminating any benchmark for comparison.

Americus Trust for Exxon Shares

As of this writing in late October 1985, shares of Exxon are being exchanged for Americus Trust Units. Exxon is one of 30 Americus stocks which will be tendered in the two year period between 1985 and 1987. Trading in the Units (ticker symbol XNU), PRIMEs (XNP), and SCOREs (XNS) began on the American Stock Exchange on a when-issued basis on September 10, 1985.

In many respects, the Americus Trust for Exxon is a test case. If successful, other Americus Trusts are likely to be successful also. If only moderately successful, the offering may serve as a door opener for the issues scheduled to follow. As of October 1985, more than 2 1/2 million shares of Exxon had been tendered.

The Exxon offer is for ten million shares. The Termination Claim was set at $60 with the stock trading around 50. The Americus Trust for Exxon will terminate in five years (September 20, 1990). In late October 1985 when Exxon common was trading at 53 3/4, the Units were priced at 54 1/4, the PRIMEs at 47 3/8, and the SCOREs at 6 7/8.

INVESTMENT STRATEGIES

SCOREs are the equivalent of warrants and all the analytical tools and techniques applicable to warrants apply equally as well to SCOREs. The only significant differences between warrants and SCOREs are (1) the absence of pitfalls caused by scheduled or unanticipated changes in terms and (2) the fact that no additional investment is required on the part of the SCORE holder to obtain any value at termination. Moreover, at termination any shares received by a SCORE holder who acquired the SCOREs when the stock was selling below the Termination Claim would represent a non-taxable event.

Trading

For reasons delineated earlier, trading SCOREs should be easier than trading warrants. These factors include the issue size, the exchange listing, the marginability, and the availability for shorting.

Hedging

SCOREs can be used in both convertible hedges and reverse hedges. The security selected to be used in conjunction with SCOREs in the hedged context will require careful consideration. When SCOREs are purchased, either the PRIME component or common stock can be used for the short position. The PRIME is desirable because of its limited appreciation potential. It is undesirable because of its high yield. When SCOREs are shorted, either the PRIME component or common stock can be used for the long position. The PRIME is desirable because of its high yield. It is undesirable because of its limited appreciation potential.

TAX CONSIDERATIONS

Recall from Chapter 11 that when warrants are exercised the holding period for the securities acquired begins on the day after the warrants are exercised. The tax rules for the Americus Trust components are considerably different.

Conversions between Units and common shares are tax free transactions; that is, deposit of shares in exchange for Units results in no tax consequences and redemption of Units for shares of common stock results in no tax consequences. In addition, the holder of either a PRIME or SCORE purchased on a day when the Termination Claim equaled or exceeded the net asset value per Unit need not recognize gain or loss upon distribution of stock when the trust terminates.

CONCLUSION

The introduction of the Americus Trusts on a large scale makes it possible to conclude this book on a very positive note. Thirty new warrants are being created and each has ideal characteristics. All of the strategies outlined in this book can be implemented in these issues without difficulty.

Although the warrant market has languished for more than ten years, it is now being given new dimensions from several sources. Those familiar with this interesting and versatile security have a great deal to anticipate in the next several years.

APPENDIX

INFORMATION SOURCES

Two advisory services are available which provide periodic coverage of the warrant markets. Both publications review an extensive list of warrants in depth and include prices, terms, and other statistics as well as recommendations for selected issues. Access to these services is virtually the only way an investor can keep abreast of new issues, changes in terms, current prices, and other relevant news. A subscription to one or both services is mandatory for the serious warrant investor.

Value Line Options & Convertibles
711 Third Avenue
New York, New York 10017

Cost: $345/year

The R.H.M. Survey of Warrants
Options & Low-Price Stocks
RHM Associates
417 Northern Boulevard
Great Neck, New York 11021

Cost: $120/year

EVALUATION OF THE VALUE LINE CONVERTIBLE SURVEY

Value Line includes coverage of approximately 75 different warrants—essentially all those for which a reasonably liquid market exists. Statistics for each issue are unusually complete including premium, volatility, and leverage calculations. In addition, Value Line has developed a proprietary mathematical evaluation model. Based on this model, Value Line calculates a fair price and the percentage by which a particular issue is undervalued or overvalued.

Value Line also ranks each warrant for performance based on the warrant statistics and factoring in also fundamentals for the underlying common stock. As a result, certain purchase and sale recommendations may be contrary to those developed in this book. For example, a well leveraged warrant with a well ranked underlying common stock might be recommended for purchase even though expiration of the warrant is pending.

EVALUATION OF THE R.H.M. SURVEY

The R.H.M. Survey covers a considerably larger number of issues including many for which only a thin market exists. Complete coverage of the Canadian market in warrants is also included.

The terms and trading basis for each issue are provided including, of course, recent prices. However, other statistics which provide the analyst with an indication of the relative merit of the warrant are lacking. The written commentary singles out issues attractive from the editor's viewpoint but for an analysis of the remaining issues the reader is left wanting.

SUMMARY

Both services suffer from the fact that prices are well over a week old by the time the compilations are in the investors' hands. It should be remembered that professional traders, market makers, and investment managers having instantaneous access to pricing information have a terrific advantage. However, many examples can be cited where warrants remained undervalued or overvalued for extended periods.

The astute investor will probably find both services necessary. However, they should be depended upon more as statistical compilations of important data than as sources of investment recommendations. In recent years the best warrant hedges were overlooked by both services.

Further, no investor should deal with warrants without being qualified as a fairly competent analyst having as a minimum mastered the principles outlined in this text. The advisory services, as well as other sources of financial information, frequently make recommendations which are at best debatable and at worst blatantly wrong. The news media in particular have printed misleading advice. The path between the warrant specialist, the financial reporter, the editor, and the cutting room is long and permits introduction of a great deal of distortion.

APPENDIX

B

STATISTICAL SUMMARY

APPENDIX B–

Common Stock					Warrant		
Ticker Symbol	Exchange	Price	Relative Volatility	Yield	Foot-Note	Listed Options	Issue
ATN	ASE	3.63	140	Nil			Acton Corp.
AXP	NYSE	45.75	100	2.8	1	✓	American Express
AGC	NYSE	35.25	75	2.8			American Gen.
ANG	ASE	8.88	135	Nil	2		Angeles Corp.
APP	NYSE	19.00	65	11.1			Apache Petrol.
AZ	NYSE	12.75	130	Nil	3		Atlas Corp.
BLY	NYSE	14.38	115	1.4	4	✓	Bally Mfg.
BKI	NYSE	5.38	150	Nil			Beker Industries
BJ	NYSE	21.00	125	2.7	5		Blair John & Co.
CAW	NYSE	13.75	140	Nil			Caesars World
CNON	OTC	19.50	130	Nil	6		Cannon Group
CHR	NYSE	2.63	190	Nil	7		Charter Co.
CODN	OTC	8.50	230	Nil			Codenoll Tech.
CF	NYSE	21.38	115	.7	8		Collins Foods Intl
COLL	OTC	4.50	190	Nil	9		Collins Industries
CHRZ	OTC	9.00	195	Nil	10		Computer Horiz.
CMTL	OTC	1.69	240	Nil	11		Comtech Inc.
CQX	ASE	8.63	130	Nil	12		Conquest Explor.
DNAP	OTC	7.38	120	Nil	13		DNA Plant Tech.
DGC	ASE	2.50	180	Nil			Digicon Inc.
DMC	NYSE	5.75	155	Nil	14		Diversified Indus.
EAL	NYSE	8.75	140	Nil			Eastern Air Lines
EAL	NYSE	8.75	140	Nil	15		Eastern Air Lines (1987 "O")
EAL	NYSE	8.75	140	Nil	16		Eastern Air Lines (1987 "A")
EMM	NYSE	8.25	150	Nil	17		Electronic Mem. & Magnetics
FMIF	OTC	6.50	190	Nil	18		FMI Financial
FPO	ASE	11.63	130	Nil	19		FPA Corp.
FCT	NYSE	13.13	125	Nil	20		Facet Enterprises
FOUR	OTC	10.00	150	.6			Forum Group Inc
FA	ASE	14.88	150	Nil	21		Frontier Holdings (Air)
FQA	NYSE	32.63	105	1.2	22		Fuqua Industries
GTI	ASE	3.00	160	Nil	23		GTI Corp
GY	NYSE	46.50	95	3.2	24		GenCorp Inc.

		Warrant—*Cont.*				Usable Security	
Exchange	Price	Conversion Ratio	Exercise Price	Expiration Date	Issue Size (Million)	Issue	Price
ASE	.38	1.150	16.48	6-01-86	.624		
ASE	36.88	2.000	27.50	2-28-87	3.502		
NYSE	15.13	1.000	24.25	1-04-89	10.560		
ASE	1.13	1.000	21.00	12-01-88	.748		
NYSE	1.38	1.000	18.00	7-15-86	6.305		
ASE	3.00	1.000	31.25	None	1.005		
ASE	3.38	1.000	40.00	1-04-88	1.111		
OTC	1.06	1.000	10.00	7-01-88	2.340	15.8s 03	95
OTC	3.33	1.000	36.75	9-15-89	2.700		
PSE	.09	1.000	24.50	8-01-85	.920	12.5s 00	100
OTC	4.25	1.000	25.00	11-01-89	2.100	12.38s 94	92
NYSE	.72	1.000	10.00	9-01-88	3.357	10.63s 98	36
OTC	2.88	.500	8.00	9-10-88	1.050		
ASE	6.38	1.000	18.17	12-15-88	1.440		
OTC	1.13	1.000	9.75	11-02-89	.480	10.5s 94	74
OTC	1.25	.500	15.25	9-20-88	.400		
OTC	.38	1.000	11.00	1-31-88	.719	13s 91	65
ASE	4.38	1.000	5.26	1-15-87	3.692		
OTC	2.00	.500	7.50	1-17-90	2.200		
ASE	.38	1.000	16.50	6-15-88	.945	12.88s 93	75
PSE	.75	1.000	9.25	5-14-86	.604		
OTC	2.00	1.000	10.00	6-01-87	2.219		
NYSE	3.50	1.000	10.00	10-15-87	4.500	$3.20 pfd.	19
NYSE	1.25	1.000	16.00	10-15-87	5.500	$3.20 pfd.	19
OTC	1.63	1.000	12.00	6-01-88	1.453	10.7s 93	86
OTC	1.44	1.000	11.38	4-29-88	7.260	9s 93	80
OTC	3.75	1.000	12.00	8-15-88	1.500	12.6s 93	82
OTC	4.25	1.000	17.00	2-15-90	.525	12.75s 00	90
OTC	3.38	2.000	9.12	12-31-85	1.089		
ASE	6.38	1.000	9.15	3-01-87	.462	5.5s 87	89
OTC	49.00	2.280	13.50	6-30-88	.602	7s 88	88
OTC	1.00	1.000	14.50	11-15-86	.430		
OTC	12.75	1.000	38.45	3-15-88	.734		

APPENDIX B—*Cont.*

	Common Stock					Warrant	
Ticker Symbol	Exchange	Price	Relative Volatility	Yield	Foot-Note	Listed Options	Issue
GCO	NYSE	5.00	150	Nil	25		Genesco
GEEN	OTC	2.25	220	Nil			Genetic Engr.
GEO	ASE	11.75	185	Nil	26		Geothermal Res.
GPO	NYSE	11.25	110	Nil	27		Giant Portland & Masonry
GNG	NYSE	12.63	130	Nil	28	✓	Golden Nugget
GTX	ASE	8.38	120	Nil			Grant Industries
GLR	NYSE	6.13	280	Nil	29		Grolier Inc.
GRIT	OTC	8.50	90	Nil	30		Grubb & Ellis REIT
HPSC	OTC	8.25	100	Nil	31		HPSC Inc.
HPH	NYSE	9.75	130	Nil	32		Harnischfeger Corp.
HOR	ASE	10.63	140	Nil	33		Horn & Hardart
ICN	NYSE	9.88	150	Nil	34		ICN Pharma-ceuticals
III	ASE	1.75	200	Nil	35		Imperial Indus.
N	NYSE	14.38	110	1.4	36		INCO Ltd.
ISY	ASE	1.88	240	Nil			Instrument Sys.
IBK	ASE	3.13	140	Nil	37		Intl. Banknote
HR	NYSE	9.13	180	Nil	38		Intl. Harvester
HR	NYSE	9.13	180	Nil			Intl. Harvester (1995 "B")
KYC	ASE	6.00	390	Nil	39		Keystone Camera Products
KDE	NYSE	33.88	85	3.5	40		Kidde Inc.
LOM	NYSE	25.38	70	10.1	41		Lomas & Nettleton
MCIC	OTC	9.38	160	Nil	42		MCI Communi-cations
MDC	NYSE	12.38	195	2.6	43		M.D.C. Corp (1988)
MDC	NYSE	12.38	195	2.6	44		M.D.C. Corp (1990)
MGM	NYSE	14.13	150	5.0	45	✓	MGM/UA Entertainment
MAT	NYSE	14.75	165	Nil			Mattel Inc.
MDR	NYSE	27.75	110	6.5	46	✓	McDermott Intl.
MII	NYSE	10.63	75	Nil	47		McLean Indus.

		Warrant—*Cont.*				Usable Security	
Exchange	Price	Conversion Ratio	Exercise Price	Expiration Date	Issue Size (Million)	Issue	Price
OTC	1.25	1.000	11.75	10-15-93	.900	9.75s 93	76
OTC	.88	1.000	5.00	10-18-86	.776		
ASE	3.13	1.000	13.50	11-15-91	.600	13s 91	101
OTC	3.50	1.000	15.00	4-15-90	.600	14.5s 95	89
NYSE	3.25	1.000	18.00	7-01-88	15.000	8.38s 93	76
ASE	1.38	1.220	14.07	7-28-86	.574		
OTC	1.88	1.000	6.00	11-01-88	2.050	13.6s 03	93
OTC	1.50	1.000	9.50	4-09-90	1.250		
OTC	2.25	1.000	11.00	1-15-89	2.500	10s 94	77
OTC	4.00	1.000	13.38	4-14-89	2.000		
ASE	2.88	1.000	18.75	12-27-87	1.728		
OTC	3.25	1.000	9.00	5-14-89	.200	12.5s 99	89
OTC	.31	1.000	4.00	3-31-87	1.319		
OTC	2.94	1.000	11.72	8-20-85	3.449		
OTC	.31	1.000	4.50	7-31-86	3.545		
ASE	.88	1.000	4.84	7-31-88	5.720	10s 98	66
NYSE	5.88	1.000	5.00	12-15-93	10.845	18s 02	114
OTC	3.44	1.000	9.00	12-31-90	7.972	13.25s95	93
OTC	1.81	1.000	8.25	3-20-90	1.000		
ASE	3.75	1.000	40.00	11-15-87	3.000		
NYSE	2.75	1.000	27.00	3-01-90	3.000		
OTC	1.25	1.000	27.50	8-01-88	36.00	9.5s 93	83
OTC	2.50	1.000	18.00	4-15-88	3.080	7s 93	77
OTC	3.50	1.000	14.10	4-15-90	5.325	10.5s 95	82
NYSE	2.88	1.000	20.00	4-14-88	2.515	10s 93	83
NYSE	10.75	1.000	4.00	4-05-86	2.902		
NYSE	7.88	1.000	25.00	4-01-90	5.999	10s 03	86
NYSE	3.63	1.000	11.20	7-15-90	8. 998	12s 03	86

APPENDIX B—*Cont.*

	Common Stock					Warrant	
Ticker Symbol	Exchange	Price	Relative Volatility	Yield	Foot-Note	Listed Options	Issue
MRT	NYSE	19.50	85	9.2	48		Mortgage & Realty Trust
MAC	ASE	8.63	180	Nil	49		Muse Air
NAUG	OTC	5.25	160	Nil	50		Naugles Inc.
NP	NYSE	1.63	170	Nil	51		Newpark Res.
NTK	NYSE	16.25	130	.5	52		Nortek Inc.
OXY	NYSE	32.00	90	7.8	53	✓	Occidental Petrol.
OPC	NYSE	11.75	180	Nil	54		Orion Pictures
OXCO	OTC	1.13	165	Nil	55		Oxoco Inc
PN	NYSE	6.25	145	Nil	56		Pan Am Corp
PNL	ASE	12.25	115	1.6	57		Penril Corp
PTL	ASE	2.88	185	Nil	58		Petro-Lewis
PIR	NYSE	19.63	135	Nil	59		Pier 1 Inc.
PNH	NYSE	4.13	110	Nil			Public Service of New Hampshire
RAI	NYSE	7.25	155	Nil			Republic Airlines
SFE	NYSE	9.00	185	Nil	60		Safeguard Sci.
SHV	ASE	5.75	165	1.4	61		Standard Havens
SEQ	NYSE	20.50	80	9.0	62		Storage Equities
SCI	NYSE	74.50	100	.5	63	✓	Storer Commun.
TCOMA	OTC	31.00	115	Nil			Tele-Commun.
TEI	NYSE	2.63	230	Nil	64		Texas Intl.
TGR	NYSE	7.88	165	Nil	65		Tiger Intl.
TPN	ASE	12.00	130	1.5	66		Total Petroleum
TW	NYSE	34.75	130	1.2		✓	Transworld (1987 A)
TRI	NYSE	27.50	100	1.5			Triangle Indus.
OIL	NYSE	25.13	125	.4	67		Triton Energy
TYL	NYSE	15.00	115	2.7	68		Tyler Corp
UNFI	OTC	11.63	165	Nil			Unifi Inc.
U	NYSE	35.00	120	.3		✓	USAir Group Inc
UH	NYSE	8.25	150	Nil	69		U.S. Home Corp
USPC	OTC	14.25	120	Nil	70		U.S. Playing Card
WCI	NYSE	27.75	125	Nil	71	✓	Warner Commun.
WBB	NYSE	21.75	145	.9	72		Web, Del E. Corp.
WAL	NYSE	6.63	150	Nil	73		Western Air Lines
WICS	OTC	3.63	180	Nil	74		Wickes Company

		Warrant—*Cont.*				Usable Security	
Exchange	Price	Conversion Ratio	Exercise Price	Expiration Date	Issue Size (Million)	Issue	Price
ASE	3.63	1.500	20.50	1-14-92	2.200		
ASE	.19	1.000	16.00	4-30-86	1.100		
OTC	1.00	1.000	12.00	4-29-89	.600	13.75s 99	86
OTC	.38	1.000	8.63	10-15-88	.550		
OTC	4.25	1.000	13.38	6-15-87	.650	15s 02	105
NYSE	12.75	1.000	25.00	4-14-87	7.700	8.95s 94	81
OTC	2.00	1.000	20.50	2-01-89	2.100	10s 94	78
OTC	.13	1.000	10.50	10-15-87	.800		
NYSE	3.00	1.000	8.00	5-01-93	10.000	13.5s 03	89
OTC	3.63	1.000	14.00	2-01-88	1.260	10.9s 93	85
ASE	.31	1.100	16.61	2-15-88	6.358	11.5s93	72
ASE	3.75	1.000	22.00	7-15-88	1.050		
OTC	1.88	1.000	5.00	10-15-91	11.119	17.5s 04	82
NYSE	1.38	1.000	10.00	5-15-86	3.740		
NYSE	1.63	1.210	12.02	6-30-87	1.491		
ASE	1.75	1.000	13.50	8-26-88	1.100		
OTC	4.75	1.000	17.00	12-04-89	2.360	9.875s 90	93
OTC	45.50	1.000	40.00	5-13-88	2.300	10s 03	78
OTC	14.75	1.030	20.53	1-01-88	5.750	11.5s 95	95
OTC	.44	1.000	8.91	7-14-88	.900	13.1s 93	58
OTC	3.25	1.000	12.50	6-30-88	3.213	8.63s 95	62
ASE	1.00	1.000	15.50	6-30-86	2.200		
NYSE	18.00	1.000	18.06	1-15-87	1.800		
OTC	13.75	1.000	18.50	9-01-93	.258	11.5s 03	79
OTC	8.25	1.000	22.00	11-15-89	1.080	13.5s 94	97
ASE	2.00	1.000	17.00	11-01-87	3.000	12.9s 94	99
OTC	5.75	1.563	11.28	7-01-88	.900	12.25s 88	100
ASE	19.25	1.040	17.31	4-01-87	.414	5.5s 87	92
OTC	2.00	1.000	9.25	4-15-90	5.000	11.3s 90	92
OTC	6.00	1.000	16.38	6-15-90	1.830	9.875s 93	73
ASE	.81	1.000	55.00	4-30-86	2.852		
OTC	4.50	1.000	26.00	4-15-88	.575	11.5s 88	97
NYSE	1.75	1.000	9.50	6-15-93	9.000	10.75s 98	77
OTC	1.50	1.000	4.43	1-26-92	11.988	11.38s 97	84

Source: Value Line Convertibles, May 27, 1985

APPENDIX B FOOTNOTES

1. Issued after April 24, 1972. Company may accelerate expiration date if common closes at or above $47.50 for ten consecutive trading days. Callable at $40.
2. Callable at $16.80. Company may accelerate expiration date by up to two years if common closes at or above $31.50 for ten consecutive trading days.
3. Not protected for stock dividends.
4. Company may accelerate expiration date if common closes at or above $72.50 for ten consecutive trading days. Callable at $32.50 after June 2, 1985.
5. Callable after September 15, 1987 if common closes at or above $55.125 for any twenty days within a thirty consecutive trading day period.
6. Callable after October 31, 1986 at $7.50 only if common closes at or above $37.50 for any twenty days within a thirty consecutive trading day period.
7. Expiration may be accelerated if common closes at $12 or above for 60 consecutive trading days. Warrant may be exchanged for $1.25 during ten trading days prior to September 1, 1988, unless already expired. Company filed for Chapter XI bankruptcy proceedings on April 20, 1984.
8. Company may accelerate expiration date by up to two years if common closes at or above $32.67 for ten consecutive trading days. Callable at $14.67.
9. Callable at $3 if common closes at or above $14.625 for twenty days within a thirty consecutive trading day period.
10. Exercisable only in multiples of two. Callable after September 19, 1986 at $.75 if common closes above 150 percent of exercise price on any twenty days within a thirty consecutive trading day period.
11. Callable at $2 after February 1, 1986 if common closes above $20 for twenty consecutive trading days.
12. Company may accelerate expiration date if common trades at or above $25 for sixty consecutive trading days.
13. Exercise price rises to $5.25 after January 17, 1987. Company reserves the right to extend life of the warrant and change the exercise price during the extended term.
14. Issued after April 24, 1972. Extended from May 14, 1983 to May 14, 1986.
15. Company may accelerate expiration to October 15, 1985 if common trades above $15 for forty-five consecutive trading days. EAL $3.20 preferred can be applied in lieu of cash at liquidation value of $21.625 a share. Preferred dividend is currently in arrears.

16. Company may accelerate expiration to October 15, 1985 if common trades at or above $24 for forty-five consecutive trading days. EAL $3.20 preferred can be applied in lieu of cash at liquidation value of $21.625 a share. Preferred dividend is currently in arrears.

17. Callable at $3 after June 1, 1986 if common closes above $18 on any twenty days within a period of thirty consecutive trading days.

18. Company may reduce exercise price at any time. At expiration unexercised warrants will be converted into 1/200 common share. Callable after May 1, 1985 if common closes above 150 percent of exercise price for any twenty days within a thirty consecutive day period.

19. Callable at $4 after August 15, 1985 if common closes above 150 percent of exercise price on any 20 days within a thirty consecutive trading day period.

20. Company may accelerate expiration date if common closes above $25.50 for twenty days within a thirty consecutive trading day period.

21. Trades as Frontier Airlines warrant.

22. Warrant's life has been extended from 1983.

23. Callable at $1 if common closes at or above 7 1/2 for twenty consecutive trading days. Company reserves the right to extend life but not beyond November 15, 1988.

24. Company may accelerate expiration date if common closes above 150 percent of exercise price for twenty days within a thirty consecutive day period. At expiration unexercised warrants will be converted into 1/100 common share.

25. Callable at $5 after October 14, 1985 only if common closes above $17.50 for twenty of thirty consecutive trading days.

26. Expiration date may be accelerated to as early as November 15, 1987 if the common closes at or above $20.25 for thirty consecutive trading days.

27. Callable at $5 before April 15, 1988 if common closes at or above $21 for twenty days within a thirty consecutive trading day period.

28. Callable at $6 if common closes above $36 for any twenty days in a thirty trading day period.

29. Company may accelerate expiration date if common closes at or above 140 percent of exercise price for 30 consecutive trading days.

30. Company may accelerate expiration date to as early as April 10, 1987 if common closes at or above $14.25 for twenty consecutive trading days. If a warrant is not exercised, it will be converted into 1/5 common share on expiration date.

31. Callable at $4 if common closes 150 percent above exercise price for twenty of thirty consecutive trading days.

32. Company may accelerate the expiration date if the common closes at or above $20.0625 on any twenty days within thirty consecutive trading days.

33. Callable at $11.11.

34. Not callable before May 15, 1987 unless common closes at or above $12.60 for any twenty days within a thirty consecutive trading day period.

35. Callable at $1 if common exceeds $4 for ten consecutive trading days. Exercise price increases to $5 after March 31, 1986.

36. Issued after April 24, 1972. All prices in U.S. dollars. Warrant exercise price is $16 (Canadian) per share. Company reserves the right to reduce exercise price.

37. Company can accelerate expiration date if common closes at or above following prices for twenty days within thirty consecutive trading day period: 200 percent of exercise price through July 31, 1985; 150 percent of exercise price August 1, 1985 through July 31, 1987; 100 percent of exercise price after August 1, 1987.

38. Company reserves the right to extend expiration date to December 15, 1999.

39. Callable at $.75 before March 20, 1987 only if common exceeds $11.55 for twenty days within a thirty consecutive trading day period. Callable at $.75 any time after March 20, 1987.

40. Company reserves the right to reduce the exercise price at any time.

41. Expiration date may be accelerated if common closes at or above $57.80 for twenty days within a thirty consecutive trading day period.

42. Callable at $8.50 on or after August 1, 1986 only if common averages 150 percent of exercise price for twenty consecutive trading days.

43. Callable at $7 if common closes above $27 on any twenty days within a thirty consecutive trading day period.

44. Not callable until April 15, 1988 unless common closes at or above $20.445 for twenty days within a thirty consecutive trading day period. First call price is $5.

45. Company reserves the right to reduce the exercise price at any time. Callable after April 14, 1986 at $5 if common closes above 150 percent of exercise price for any twenty days within a thirty consecutive day period.

46. Company can accelerate the expiration date to April 1, 1988 if common is at least 125 percent of exercise price for twenty days within a thirty consecutive trading day period. Company has the right to reduce the exercise price by 1/3 at any time.

47. Callable at $3 after July 15, 1988 if common closes above 150 percent of exercise price on any twenty days in a thirty consecutive trading day period. Company reserves the right to reduce the exercise price at any time.

48. Callable at $3 before January 15, 1991 only if common closes at or above $28.70 for twenty days within a thirty consecutive trading day period.

49. Company may accelerate expiration if common trades above 150 percent of exercise price for thirty consecutive trading days. Company has agreed to a merger.

50. Not callable before April 30, 1987 unless common closes at or above $16.80 for any twenty days within a thirty consecutive trading day period. Callable after April 30, 1987 at $5.

51. Company may accelerate the expiration date to as early as October 15, 1985 if common closes at or above $12.9375 for thirty consecutive trading days.

52. Issued after April 24, 1972. Callable after June 14, 1985 at $3.25. Company reserves the right to accelerate the expiration if common closes above $20 for twenty consecutive trading days.

53. Not exercisable until January 1, 1986. After that date the warrants can also be exchanged for common shares without any additional payment at a ratio of 5 warrants for 2 common shares.

54. Company may accelerate expiration date if common closes 140 percent above exercise price for twenty of thirty consecutive trading days.

55. Callable after October 15, 1985 at $5.25.

56. Company may accelerate expiration to May 1, 1988 if common closes at or above $10 for thirty consecutive trading days. Callable at $3 after May 1, 1986 if common closes at or above $10 for thirty consecutive trading days.

57. Callable at $2 after February 1, 1986 if common closes above $21 for twenty consecutive trading days. At expiration each warrant will be converted into 1/100 share.

58. Callable at $2.95 after February 14, 1986 if common closes above $25 for any thirty trading days within a forty-five consecutive trading day period.

59. Callable at $18. Company may accelerate expiration to July 15, 1986 if common is at least $40 for ten consecutive trading days. Company may extend life of warrant up to two years on three occasions with an increase of $.50 in the exercise price.

60. Issued after April 24, 1972. Company has extended life of warrant from June 30, 1984 to June 30, 1987. Callable at $10.50.

61. Callable at $10.50. Company may accelerate expiration date up to twenty-four months if common closes at or above $24 for ten consecutive trading days.

62. Callable at $2.50 if common closes at or above $25.50 for twenty days within a thirty consecutive trading day period.

63. Callable at $10 after May 14, 1986 if common closes above $60 on any twenty trading days within a period of thirty consecutive trading days. Company has agreed to a leveraged buyout.

64. Callable at $3.50 after July 14, 1986 only if common is a least 150 percent of exercise price on any twenty days within a thirty consecutive trading day period.

65. Callable at $2 after July 1, 1985 if common closes at or above 150 percent of exercise price for ten consecutive trading days. The 11.5s95 sinking fund debenture is also usable at par to exercise the warrant. Interest on bonds payable in cash or common shares. Payment dated April 1, 1985 was in stock.

66. Dealings are only in multiples of ten warrants.

67. Callable at $6.375 after November 15, 1986 only if common closes at or above $30.80 for 20 days within a thirty consecutive trading day period.

68. Callable before November 1, 1985 at $2.50 only if common trades at or above $25 for any twenty days within a thirty consecutive trading day period. Callable at $2.50 at any time after November 1, 1985.

69. Callable at $2 after April 15, 1987 if common closes at or above $13.875 for twenty days within a thirty consecutive trading day period.

70. Callable before June 15, 1986 if common closes at or above $24.50 for any twenty days in a thirty consecutive trading day period. Exercise price adjusted June 15, 1986 to 80 percent of the average closing price of the common for sixty consecutive trading days ending May 15, 1986 but not above $16.375 or below $7.

71. Issued after April 24, 1972. Company can accelerate the expiration date if stock closes above $100 for ten consecutive trading days. Callable at $45.

72. Callable at $5 after May 1, 1987 if common trades above $39 for any twenty days within thirty consecutive trading days. At expiration each warrant will be converted into 1/100 share common.

73. Callable at $3 after June 14, 1986 if common closes at or above $11.875 for thirty consecutive days. Company may accelerate expiration if common closes at or above $11.875 for thirty consecutive trading days.

74. Company may accelerate expiration date up to forty-eight months if common closes at or above $8.86 for ten consecutive trading days. Callable at $4.43 after January 26, 1987.

APPENDIX

C

CUMULATIVE NORMAL DISTRIBUTION

The cumulative normal density function $N(d)$ is a statistical concept. It is the area under the normal curve below d. In the Black-Scholes model, the stock's return is assumed to be log-normally distributed; therefore, $N(d)$ is the probability that, in a normal distribution, a deviation less than d will occur. Tables for the cumulative normal distribution model are included in most mathematical handbooks and statistical texts. An abbreviated table is provided in Exhibit 6A-1.

From the sample solution for the Black-Scholes model given in Exhibit 6-12, $d_1 = .417$ and $d_2 = -.072$. Using the table in Exhibit 6A-1, $N(d_1) \approx .662$ and $N(d_2) \approx .472$.

The function $N(d)$ can also be calculated using the following approximation.[1] Programed into a computer of pocket calculator, this formula permits a rapid solution of the Black-Scholes model. Using the mathematical approximation, Exhibit 6A-2 shows calculations for the values of $N(d_1)$ and $N(d_2)$ required for the sample solution of the Black-Scholes model given in Exhibit 6-12.

or pocket calculator, this formula permits a rapid solution of the Black-Scholes model. Using the mathematical approximation, Exhibit C-1 shows calculations for the values of $N(d_1)$ and $N(d_2)$ required for the sample solution of the Black-Scholes model given in Exhibit 6-12.

$$N(d) = \left[1 - \left(\frac{1}{\sqrt{2\pi}}e^{-d^2/2}\right)(.4361836k\right.$$
$$\left. - .1201676k^2 + .9372980k^3)\right]$$

$$= \left[1 - (.3989)(e^{-d^2/2})(.4361836k\right.$$
$$\left. - .1201676k^2 + .9372980k^3)\right] \tag{C-1}$$

$$k = \frac{1}{1 + .33267d} \tag{C-2}$$

EXHIBIT C-1
Solving for N(d) Using a Mathematical Approximation

Equation Variable: $d_1 = .417$

Solution for $N(d_1)$: $k_1 = \dfrac{1}{1 + (.33267)(.417)}$

$$= .8781764$$

$$k_1^2 = .7711938$$

$$k_1^3 = .6772442$$

$$e^{-d^2/2} = .9167$$

$$N(d_1) = 1 - (.3989)(.9167)\Big[(.4361)(.8782)$$

$$- (.1202)(.7712) + (.9373)(.6772)\Big]$$

$$= 1 - (.3657)(.9252)$$

Answer: $N(d_1) = .662$

Equation Variable: $d_2 = -.0722$

Solution for $N(d_2)$: $k_2 = \dfrac{1}{1 + (.33267)(-0.0722)}$

$$= 1.0246099$$

$$k_2^2 = 1.0498254$$

$$k_2^3 = 1.0756615$$

$$e^{-d^2/2} = .9974$$

$$N(d_2) = 1 - (.3989)(.9974)\Big[(.4361)(1.0246)$$

$$- (.1202)(1.0498) + (.9373)(1.0757)\Big]$$

$$= 1 - (.3979)(1.329)$$

Answer: $N(d_2) = .472$

EXHIBIT C-2
Cumulative Normal Probability Distribution Where d_1 or d_2 is Positive

d	.00	.01	.02	.03	.04	.05	.06	.07	.08	.09
0.00	.5000	.5040	.5080	.5120	.5159	.5199	.5239	.5279	.5319	.5358
0.10	.5398	.5438	.5478	.5517	.5557	.5596	.5636	.5675	.5714	.5753
0.20	.5793	.5832	.5871	.5909	.5948	.5987	.6026	.6064	.6103	.6141
0.30	.6179	.6217	.6255	.6293	.6331	.6368	.6406	.6443	.6480	.6517
0.40	.6554	.6591	.6628	.6664	.6700	.6736	.6772	.6808	.6844	.6879
0.50	.6915	.6950	.6985	.7019	.7054	.7088	.7123	.7157	.7190	.7224
0.60	.7257	.7291	.7324	.7356	.7389	.7421	.7454	.7486	.7517	.7549
0.70	.7580	.7611	.7642	.7673	.7703	.7734	.7764	.7793	.7823	.7852
0.80	.7881	.7910	.7939	.7967	.7995	.8023	.8051	.8078	.8106	.8133
0.90	.8159	.8186	.8212	.8238	.8264	.8289	.8315	.8340	.8365	.8389
1.00	.8413	.8437	.8461	.8485	.8508	.8531	.8554	.8577	.8599	.8621
1.10	.8643	.8665	.8686	.8708	.8729	.8749	.8770	.8790	.8810	.8830
1.20	.8849	.8869	.8888	.8906	.8925	.8943	.8962	.8980	.8997	.9015
1.30	.9032	.9049	.9066	.9082	.9099	.9115	.9131	.9147	.9162	.9177

1.40	.9192	.9207	.9222	.9236	.9251	.9265	.9279	.9292	.9306	.9319
1.50	.9332	.9345	.9357	.9370	.9382	.9394	.9406	.9418	.9429	.9441
1.60	.9452	.9463	.9474	.9484	.9495	.9505	.9515	.9525	.9535	.9545
1.70	.9554	.9564	.9573	.9582	.9591	.9599	.9608	.9616	.9625	.9633
1.80	.9641	.9649	.9656	.9664	.9671	.9678	.9686	.9693	.9699	.9706
1.90	.9713	.9719	.9726	.9732	.9738	.9744	.9750	.9756	.9761	.9767
2.00	.9772	.9778	.9783	.9788	.9793	.9798	.9803	.9808	.9812	.9817
2.10	.9821	.9826	.9830	.9834	.9838	.9842	.9846	.9850	.9854	.9857
2.20	.9861	.9864	.9868	.9871	.9875	.9878	.9881	.9884	.9887	.9890
2.30	.9893	.9896	.9898	.9901	.9904	.9906	.9909	.9911	.9913	.9916
2.40	.9918	.9920	.9922	.9925	.9927	.9929	.9931	.9932	.9934	.9936
2.50	.9938	.9940	.9941	.9943	.9945	.9946	.9948	.9949	.9951	.9952
2.60	.9953	.9955	.9956	.9957	.9959	.9960	.9961	.9962	.9963	.9964
2.70	.9965	.9966	.9967	.9968	.9969	.9970	.9971	.9972	.9973	.9974
2.80	.9974	.9975	.9976	.9977	.9977	.9978	.9979	.9979	.9980	.9981
2.90	.9981	.9982	.9982	.9983	.9984	.9984	.9985	.9985	.9986	.9986
3.00	.9986	.9987	.9987	.9988	.9988	.9989	.9989	.9989	.9990	.9990

EXHIBIT C-2 *Continued*

Cumulative Normal Probability Distribution Where d_1 or d_2 is Negative

d	.00	.01	.02	.03	.04	.05	.06	.07	.08	.09
−3.00	.0014	.0013	.0013	.0012	.0012	.0011	.0011	.0011	.0010	.0010
−2.90	.0019	.0018	.0018	.0017	.0016	.0016	.0015	.0015	.0014	.0014
−2.80	.0026	.0025	.0024	.0023	.0023	.0022	.0021	.0021	.0020	.0019
−2.70	.0035	.0034	.0033	.0032	.0031	.0030	.0029	.0028	.0027	.0026
−2.60	.0047	.0045	.0044	.0043	.0041	.0040	.0039	.0038	.0037	.0036
−2.50	.0062	.0060	.0059	.0057	.0055	.0054	.0052	.0051	.0049	.0048
−2.40	.0082	.0080	.0078	.0075	.0073	.0071	.0069	.0068	.0066	.0064
−2.30	.0107	.0104	.0102	.0099	.0096	.0094	.0091	.0089	.0087	.0084
−2.20	.0139	.0136	.0132	.0129	.0125	.0122	.0119	.0116	.0113	.0110
−2.10	.0179	.0174	.0170	.0166	.0162	.0158	.0154	.0150	.0146	.0143
−2.00	.0228	.0222	.0217	.0212	.0207	.0202	.0197	.0192	.0188	.0183
−1.90	.0287	.0281	.0274	.0268	.0262	.0256	.0250	.0244	.0239	.0233
−1.80	.0359	.0351	.0344	.0336	.0329	.0322	.0314	.0307	.0301	.0294
−1.70	.0446	.0436	.0427	.0418	.0409	.0401	.0392	.0384	.0375	.0367
−1.60	.0548	.0537	.0526	.0516	.0505	.0495	.0485	.0475	.0465	.0455

	.0668	.0655	.0643	.0630	.0618	.0606	.0594	.0582	.0571	.0559
−1.50	.0668	.0655	.0643	.0630	.0618	.0606	.0594	.0582	.0571	.0559
−1.40	.0808	.0793	.0778	.0764	.0749	.0735	.0721	.0708	.0694	.0681
−1.30	.0968	.0951	.0934	.0918	.0901	.0885	.0869	.0853	.0838	.0823
−1.20	.1151	.1131	.1112	.1094	.1075	.1057	.1038	.1020	.1003	.0985
−1.10	.1357	.1335	.1314	.1292	.1271	.1251	.1230	.1210	.1190	.1170
−1.00	.1587	.1563	.1539	.1515	.1492	.1469	.1446	.1423	.1401	.1379
−0.90	.1841	.1814	.1788	.1762	.1736	.1711	.1685	.1660	.1635	.1611
−0.80	.2119	.2090	.2061	.2033	.2005	.1977	.1949	.1922	.1894	.1867
−0.70	.2420	.2389	.2358	.2327	.2297	.2266	.2236	.2207	.2177	.2148
−0.60	.2743	.2709	.2676	.2644	.2611	.2579	.2546	.2514	.2483	.2451
−0.50	.3085	.3050	.3015	.2981	.2946	.2912	.2877	.2843	.2810	.2776
−0.40	.3446	.3409	.3372	.3336	.3300	.3264	.3228	.3192	.3156	.3121
−0.30	.3821	.3783	.3745	.3707	.3669	.3632	.3594	.3557	.3520	.3483
−0.20	.4207	.4168	.4129	.4091	.4052	.4013	.3974	.3936	.3897	.3859
−0.10	.4602	.4562	.4522	.4483	.4443	.4404	.4364	.4325	.4286	.4247
−0.00	.5000	.4960	.4920	.4880	.4841	.4801	.4761	.4721	.4681	.4642

Source: Labuszewski, John and Sinquefield, Jeanne Cairns. *Inside the Commodity Option Markets.* New York: John Wiley & Sons, Inc., 1985.

APPENDIX

D

GLOSSARY

Adjusted exercise price: The exercise price per share of the underlying security. Traded warrants are frequently options on fractional or multiple shares, and the exercise price may be stated as the total exercise price, the amount which must be submitted to convert the warrant into all the shares which it represents.

Adjusted warrant price: The price of a warrant for a single share of the underlying security. It is the market price of the warrant divided by the number of shares receivable upon exercise.

American option: A put or call option that can be exercised at any time prior to expiration. This is in contrast to a European option which can be exercised only on the expiration date. The distinction is important to theoreticians since the latter is usually easier to analyze. All listed options traded in the United States are American options.

Americus Trust: A unit investment trust authorized to issue Units in exchange for validly tendered shares of eligible securities. The Units are divisible into two parts, the PRIME component which entitles holders to the income from the underlying shares and the SCORE component which entitles holders to the appreciation from the underlying shares.

Anti-dilution clause: A provision in the warrant agreement providing an adjustment in warrant terms in the event of stock splits, stock dividends, or the sale of new stock. As a result the warrant value is not impacted by any of the above events and the warrant holder's proportionate claim to equity in the issuing company remains unchanged.

Appreciation multiple: A value indicator used to determine the attractiveness of a warrant by comparing relative performance of warrant positions vis-à-vis stock positions.

Arbitrage: The simultaneous purchase and sale of identical, substantially identical, or equivalent assets in one or more than one market with the intent of capturing the price differential as a riskless profit.

Asked: The price at which an asset can be acquired from a potential seller. The asked price is usually quoted with the bid price, the price at which an asset can be sold to a potential buyer. The difference between the bid price and the asked price is known as the spread.

Assignment: Notification to a writer by the Options Clearing Corporation that the terms of an option contract must be fulfilled. For a call writer this is an obligation to sell stock at the exercise price. For a put seller this is an obligation to buy stock at the exercise price.

Attached: A description for warrants which have not been separated from the securities with which they were originally issued.

At-the-money: The price relationship where the exercise price of the option (warrant) is equal to the market price of the underlying instrument.

Beta: A numerical measure of the sensitivity of movements in the price of a stock to movements in the overall market as reflected by a broad-based index such as the S&P 500 or the NYSE Composite Index. A beta of 1.10 indicates that the stock will rise or fall 10 percent more than a corresponding move in the market.

Bid: The price at which an asset can be sold to a potential buyer. The bid price is usually quoted with the asked price, the price at which an asset can be purchased from a potential seller. The difference between the bid price and the asked price is known as the spread.

Black-Scholes formula: A mathematical model derived from option theory used to calculate the price at which an option *should* trade. The formula can be applied to warrants as well. The model is one means of determining fair value.

Breakeven point: The stock price (or prices) at which an investment strategy produces zero net gain or loss.

Breakeven time: A value indicator for a convertible security. It is the time it would take for the premium over conversion value to be erased by the convertible's yield advantage. Expressed mathematically, it is the conversion premium in dollars divided by the convertible income advantage in dollars.

Bullish: A market outlook anticipating rising prices.

Buy-in: An involuntary repurchase of shares previously sold short because of the inability of the brokerage firm to borrow the shares necessary to retain the short position.

Bearish: A market outlook anticipating declining prices.

Callable: A provision giving the issuer the right to redeem warrants at a specified price. Warrants are usually called when the intrinsic value exceeds the call price thereby forcing conversion.

Call option: A contract granting the privilege but not the obligation to purchase an asset at a specified price for a specified period after which the contract is worthless. A warrant is one variation of a call option.

Closed-end fund: See publicly-traded fund.

Closing price: The last price at which transactions are made prior to the closing bell.

Closing purchase transaction: Termination of a short option position by an offsetting purchase.

Closing sale transaction: Termination of a long option position by an offsetting sale.

Closing transaction: The termination of an open position by its corresponding offset. For option buyers this transaction is a closing sale. For option sellers this transaction is a closing purchase.

Collateral: Cash or securities (including T-bills) deposited with a broker to guarantee performance on short positions (stocks and options).

Contingent claim: A term used interchangeably for an option or any security having the features of an option such as a warrant, convertible bond, or convertible preferred stock. Fulfillment of these contracts requires performance by both parties involved. The option grantor has the liability to deliver stock in the case of calls (warrants) or to receive stock in the case of puts. Those obligations are contingent upon conditions which the buyer must meet; namely, paying the exercise price in the case of calls or delivering stock in the case of puts.

Conversion ratio: The number of units of the optioned security obtainable with each traded warrant.

Convertible hedge: A strategy combining the purchase of undervalued warrants with the short sale of stock or other securities to capture as profit a relative warrant undervaluation.

Convertible security: Bonds or preferred stock with special provision that they can be exchanged for other securities—usually a common stock issue—at the holder's request. Technically, options and warrants are also convertible securities.

Cover: To buy back as a closing transaction a security which was previously sold.

Covered writing: An investment strategy in which common stock is purchased and call options are sold on a one-for-one basis.

Credit: A positive account balance resulting from any transaction bringing money into an account such as a deposit or an option opening sale transaction.

Debenture with warrants: A debt issue which has a fixed number of warrants attached. Usually the warrants can be detached after a specified date, and separate trading markets develop for the bonds with warrants attached, for the stripped bonds, and for the warrants. Frequently the bonds have the provision that they can be used at face value in lieu of cash when exercising the warrants.

Deep-in-the-money: An alternative description for options (warrants) having substantial intrinsic value. For calls and warrants it is the price relationship where the stock price is far above the exercise price. For puts it is the condition where the stock price is well below the exercise price.

Delayed convertible: A warrant or other convertible security with terms prohibiting immediate conversion. Conversion is permitted only after a specified future date.

Delivery: The transfer of securities when an option (warrant) is exercised.

Discount option: An option (warrant) selling below its intrinsic value. The premium plus the exercise price is less than the price of the underlying security.

Downside breakeven: The price below which an investment strategy generates losses.

Downside protection: The cushion against falling prices provided by the premium received from the sale of call options.

Dual-purpose fund: A publicly-traded (closed-end) investment company offering two classes of securities—income shares and capital shares. Holders of the income shares receive all the interest and dividends on the underlying portfolio while holders of the capital shares receive all the gains or losses.

Early exercise: The exercise of an option (warrant) prior to its expiration date.

Equity-linked security: Any security whose value is dependent upon the price of the underlying common stock. Included would be warrants, convertible bonds, convertible preferred stocks, and options.

European option: A put or call that can be exercised only on the expiration date. In contrast to an American option which can be exercised at any time prior to expiration.

Exercise: The process of submitting a warrant with the required exercise price (usually cash) in exchange for the underlying security. For options the process is slightly different. In the case of calls exercise entails purchase of stock from the writer. In the case of puts exercise entails sale of stock to the writer.

Exercise price: The amount which must be submitted with each option (warrant) to obtain the optioned security.

Expiration date: The day on which the option (warrant) contract terminates and thereafter becomes null and void. For listed options the expiration date is the Saturday following the third Friday of the month. For warrants the expiration date is not standardized.

Extrinsic value: The value of an option (warrant) over and above the intrinsic value. Extrinsic value is also called time value. The price of an out-of-the-money option (warrant) is entirely extrinsic value.

Ex-warrants: A description for senior securities, originally issued with warrants, from which the warrants have been detached. These issues trade at a price reflecting investment merit which is independent of the warrant price. Such bonds are often quoted "xw".

Fair value: The price at which an option (warrant) should trade in an efficient market as predicted by theory.

Forced conversion: Exercise of a warrant necessitated by the issuer's decision to invoke the call provision. Warrants are called when the intrinsic value exceeds the call price. Under these conditions warrant holders would incur substantial loss by tendering rather than converting. By forcing conversion the issuer gets an influx of cash (the exercise price) and eliminates the warrants from the capital structure. Depending upon the price, usable bonds may also be eliminated from the capital structure at the same time.

Gamma factor: A parameter which enables precise determination of a warrant's price track. It is one component of a mathematical formula derived through solution of Samuelson's warrant model.

Hedge: A combination of long and short positions in related securities (which are relatively mispriced) designed to capture the undervaluation or overvaluation as profit while at the same time providing considerably less risk than a position in the individual securities.

Hedge ratio: A calculation—namely, the number of warrants sold short divided by the number of common shares held long—which characterizes the investment risk and reward for a reverse warrant hedge.

Historical volatility: Volatility measured from a sequence of past stock prices.

Holder: The owner of a security.

Implied volatility: That value of volatility which, when inserted into an option model, produces a solution which is the current traded price of the option. It is the volatility which the market currently assigns to the underlying instrument.

Initial margin requirement: The minimum margin which must be posted when entering an investment position.

Institution: A large organization which commands vast resources and which trades in large volume such as a pension fund, mutual fund, bank, or insurance company.

In-the-money: An option (warrant) having intrinsic value. Call options and warrants are in-the-money when the price of the underlying instrument is above the exercise price. Put options are in-the-money when the price of the underlying instrument is below the exercise price.

Intrinsic value: The cash value of an option (warrant). It is that amount which, when combined with the exercise price, can be applied in acquiring the underlying asset. For calls (warrants) the intrinsic value is the stock price minus the exercise price. For puts the intrinsic value is the exercise price minus the stock price. In other words, it is the amount by which an option (warrant) is in-the-money.

Kicker: See "sweetener".

Latent warrant: That value of a convertible security over and above its straight bond or preferred value which can be attributed to the conversion feature. This component of a convertible has the features of a warrant and can be analyzed in a similar manner.

Leg-in: Nonsimultaneous execution of transactions in a multiple position strategy. The objective is to establish one portion and to complete others at more favorable prices.

Leverage: The magnification of the potential (both risk and reward) of an investment when a given amount of money controls assets of substantially greater value.

Leverage indicator: A value indicator used for estimating the investment potential of a warrant. It is defined as the stock price divided by the warrant price. It is that portion of the current stock price represented by warrant ownership.

Leverage ratio: A value indicator used for estimating the investment potential of a warrant. It is the percentage change in the price of a warrant resulting from a price change (usually 100 percent) in the underlying stock.

Limit order: An order to buy or sell at a specified price or better.

Liquid market: A market characterized by high volume of trading, narrow spreads, and depth (meaningful size at both bid and asked prices). Buying and selling in quantity can be accomplished without perturbing prices.

Listed options: A put or call with standardized terms traded on a national securities exchange.

Long: A position of ownership resulting from acquisition of an asset. An investor who is long will make money if the asset rises in price. As opposed to short.

Margin: The equity which must be posted by an investor to collateralize an investment position.

Mathematical advantage: A value indicator used for estimating the investment potential of a warrant. It is a reward/risk ratio obtained by comparing stock-warrant performance in a rising market scenario versus stock-warrant performance in a falling market scenario.

Maximum value: The highest rational price possible for a warrant. It is at all times equal to the current price of the optioned security.

Minimum value: Same as intrinsic value.

Model: A mathematical formula derived from the theory of options and finance the solution of which gives the price at which an option (warrant) should trade.

Neutral: A market outlook anticipating relatively unchanged prices.

Neutral hedge: A hedge balanced to give highest return when the underlying asset remains unchanged. The upside and downside breakeven points are generally equidistant from the entry price.

Offsetting transaction: A transaction which terminates an option position either long or short. An opening sale transaction is offset by a closing purchase. An opening purchase is offset by a closing sale.

Opening purchase transaction: A trade establishing a long position in an option, either a put or a call.

Opening sale transaction: A trade establishing a short position in an option, either a put or a call.

Opening transaction: A transaction establishing a new option position. An opening purchase adds a long position. An opening sale adds a short position.

Option: A contract granting the privilege but not the obligation to buy or sell at a particular price for a specified period of time.

Option period: The lifetime of the option as specified in the contract and within which the buyer must exercise or lose the privilege.

Out-of-the-money: An option (warrant) for which the intrinsic value is zero. Call options (warrants) are out-of-the-money when the price of the underlying instrument is below the exercise price. Put options are out-of-the-money when the price of the underlying instrument is above the exercise price.

Overvalued: Selling in excess of the expected price as predicted by experience or a valuation model.

Parity: The market price for an in-the-money option (warrant) that is equal to its intrinsic value. The time value of the option (warrant) is zero.

Perpetual warrant: A warrant with no expiration date. The warrants have infinite duration and can be exercised at any time in the future.

Premium: The excess of a warrant's traded price over its intrinsic value—expressed either as a dollar amount or as a percentage. In other words, it is the warrant's time value. Infrequently the term is used interchangeably with price.

PRIME: One of two components of the Americus Trust Unit. The acronym stands for "Prescribed Right to Income and Maximum Equity." PRIMEs entitle holders to the income stream from the underlying stock plus limited capital appreciation as established by the Termination Claim.

Profit profile: A graph or table showing projected returns for an investment strategy over a range of prices in the underlying instrument.

Publicly-traded fund: An investment management company which issues a fixed number of shares. Shares are not redeemable at the shareholders option as is the case with conventional mutual funds. Instead, they are purchased and sold through secondary market transactions.

Put: An option granting the holder the right but not the obligation to sell the underlying instrument at a particular price for a specified period of time.

Return: The total change in value of an investment including appreciation and yield (dividends and interest).

Return on investment: The change in value of an asset (including dividends or interest) usually expressed as a percentage of the initial investment.

Reverse hedge: A strategy combining the short sale of expiring warrants with the purchase of other related securities designed to capture as profit a relative warrant overpricing within a known time period.

Rolling: Repositioning by switching from one option into another having a different exercise price or expiration date. See also rolling up, rolling down, and rolling forward.

Rolling down: The simultaneous closing of an option position at one strike price and opening of a substantially identical position at a lower strike price.

Rolling forward: The simultaneous closing of an option position in one expiration month and opening of a substantially identical position in an expiration month further out.

Rolling up: The simultaneous closing of an option position at one strike price and opening of a substantially identical position at a higher strike price.

SCORE: One of two components of the Americus Trust Unit. The acronym stands for "Special Claim On Residual Equity." SCOREs entitle holders to the capital appreciation in the underlying stock above the level set by the Termination Claim.

Securities and Exchange Commission (SEC):   An agency of the federal government which regulates and oversees the securities markets in the United States.

Senior securities usable at par in lieu of cash: A debt instrument which can be substituted for the cash which must be submitted when exercising a warrant. Regardless of market price, the usable bond is valued at par when it is tendered in the exercise process.

Short interest: The total number of shares sold short for a particular issue. These statistics are reported monthly by the New York Stock Exchange and the American Stock Exchange for every issue in which the short interest is significant.

Short option position: The position of the writer or seller of a put or call.

Short sale: The sale of a borrowed security in anticipation of falling prices. If the drop materializes the securities are repurchased (covered) at the lower level, and the profit is the difference between the original sale price and the subsequent purchase price.

Short squeeze: A condition during which short sellers are buying in unison. It is usually triggered by bullish news or by a price increase in an issue having a large short interest. Since short sellers face potentially unlimited losses, near panic conditions may develop in their rush to cover. Since this buying puts additional upward pressure on the stock price, their condition deteriorates even further. As a final blow, investors with long positions become sellers to capitalize on the higher prices. The brokers have loaned these shares to the short sellers, and if they cannot locate additional shares to borrow they may direct a "buy-in" which causes still further distortion in the stock price.

Specialist: An exchange member responsible for making markets in specific securities and for keeping the book of public orders. This entails maintaining a liquid and continuous market buying and selling for his own account in the absence of public orders.

Speculator: An investor willing to assume excessive risk in search of disproportionate capital gain.

Standard deviation: A statistical calculation which measures the degree to which the data in a distribution cluster about a mean value.

Step-up in exercise price: A feature typical of many warrants providing for an increase—often periodic—in the future exercise price.

Strike price: The price at which the underlying asset will change hands when an option (warrant) is exercised. Also called the exercise price.

Stripped bonds: Bonds originally issued with warrants from which the warrants have been detached. Stripped bonds are also referred to as bonds trading ex-warrants.

Sweetener: A special provision (such as a warrant) added to an otherwise conventional security. It alters the terms of the issue and influences marketability because the clientele changes. Also called a "kicker".

Tangible value: (Also called minimum value or conversion value). Represents the value of the warrant in the conversion process. Mathematically it equals the current stock price less the warrant exercise price.

Termination claim: One of the specifications of an Americus Trust. It is the crossover point below which the PRIME component accrues the appreciation in the underlying stock and above which the SCORE component accrues the appreciation in the underlying stock. The Termination Claim is equivalent to the exercise price or strike price for a warrant or a call option.

Termination date: One of the specifications of an Americus Trust. It is that time when the trust is dissolved and the holders of Units, PRIMEs, and SCOREs receive a pro-rata portion of the trust assets as determined by the stock price and the termination claim.

Terms: The provisions of an option (warrant) contract including the underlying instrument, the exercise price, the expiration date, and the method of settlement.

Theoretical value: The price of an option (warrant) as computed by a valuation model.

Time value: That component of option (warrant) premium which exceeds intrinsic value. It is the amount by which the market price of an option (warrant) exceeds the amount that could be realized if the option (warrant) were exercised.

Track: An alternate term for the warrant price curve.

Transaction costs: Charges associated with executing a trade including commissions and exchange fees. It also includes a penalty imposed by the existence of the bid-asked spread.

Underlying security: The asset which can be purchased or sold in accordance with the terms of the option (warrant) contract.

Undervalued: Selling at a price below that predicted by a valuation model.

Unit: The security received from an Americus Trust in exchange for validly tendered shares of eligible securities. Units can be divided into

APPENDIX
E

BIBLIOGRAPHY

BOOKS ON WARRANTS

1. Arnold Bernhard & Co. *More Profit and Less Risk—Convertible Securities and Warrants.* New York: Arnold Bernhard & Co., 1970.
2. Auster, Rolf, *Option Writing and Hedging Strategies.* Hicksville, New York: Exposition Press, 1975.
3. Brealey, Richard and Myers, Stewart. *Principles of Corporate Finance.* New York: McGraw-Hill, 1981.
4. Cox, John C. and Rubinstein, Mark. *Options Markets.* New York: Prentice-Hall, 1985.
5. Fried, Sidney. *Fortune Building in the 70's with Common Stock Warrants and Low-Price Stocks.* New York: R.H.M. Press, 1974.
6. Fried, Sidney. *Speculating with Warrants.* New York: R.H.M. Press, 1971.
7. Fried, Sidney. *The Speculative Merits of Common Stock Warrants.* New York: R.H.M. Press, 1957.
8. Gastineau, Gary L. *The Stock Options Manual.* Second Edition. New York: McGraw-Hill, 1979.

9. Kalb, Voorhis & Co. *A Handbook to Convertible Securities*. New York: Kalb, Voorhis & Co., 1971.

10. Kassouf, Sheen T. *Evaluation of Convertible Securities*. Revised Version. New York: Analytical Publishers Co., 1969.

11. Kassouf, Sheen T. *A Theory and Econometric Model for Common Stock Purchase Warrants*. New York: Analytical Publishers, 1965.

12. Liebowitz, Martin L. and Kopprasch, Robert W. *Contingent Takedown Options on Fixed-Income Securities*. New York: Salomon Brothers, Bond Portfolio Analysis Group, January 30, 1981.

13. Mayo, Herbert B. *Using the Leverage in Warrants and Calls to Build a Successful Investment Program*. Larchmont, New York: Investors Intelligence Inc., 1974.

14. Miller, Jarrott T. *The Long and Short of Hedging*. Chicago: Henry Regnery Company, 1973.

15. Noddings, Thomas C. *The Dow Jones-Irwin Guide to Convertible Securities*. Homewood, Illinois: Dow Jones-Irwin, 1973.

16. Noddings, Thomas C. *How the Experts Beat the Market*. Homewood, Illinois: Dow Jones-Irwin, 1976.

17. Noddings, Thomas C. *Low Risk Strategies for the High Performance Investor*. Chicago: Probus Publishing, 1985.

18. Prendergast, S. Lawrence. *Uncommon Profits through Stock Purchase Warrants*. Homewood, Illinois: Dow Jones-Irwin, 1973.

19. Rorro, Thomas A. *Assessing Risk on Wall Street*. Annandale, Virginia: SOBARO Publishing Company, 1984.

20. Schwartz, William. *Using Warrants for Leverage*. Hempstead, New York: Investing and Management Compass Inc., 1967.

21. Schwartz, William and Spellman, Julius. *Guide to Convertible Securities*. New York: William Schwartz and Julius Spellman, 1968.

22. Stark, Brian J. *Special Situation Investing—Hedging, Arbitrage and Liquidation*. Homewood, Illinois: Dow Jones-Irwin, 1983.

23. Tennican, Michael L. *Convertible Debentures and Related Securities*. Cambridge, Massachusetts: Harvard University Press, 1975.

24. Thorp, Edward O. and Kassouf, Sheen T. *Beat the Market—A Scientific Stock Market System*. New York: Random House, 1967.

ARTICLES ON WARRANTS

25. Anreder, Steven S. "Not Just for Swingers—Warrants Lately Have Become Almost Respectable." *Barron's* (December 7, 1970): 5.

26. Armstrong, Thomas H. "Stock Option Warrants—Caveats for the Speculator." *The Analysts Journal* (May 1954).

27. Ayres, Herbert F. "Risk Aversion in the Warrant Markets." *Industrial Management Review* 5, No. 1 (Fall 1963).

28. Berton, Lee. "Wall Street Craze: Warrants to Buy Stocks Stir Hot Controversy But Win Big Following." *The Wall Street Journal* (May 5, 1969): 1.

29. Bierman, Harold, Jr. "The Cost of Warrants." *Journal of Financial and Quantitative Analysis* (June 1973).

30. Black, Fischer and Scholes, Myron. "The Pricing of Options and Corporate Liabilities." *Journal of Political Economy* 81 (May 1973): 637-659.

31. Chen, Andrew H. Y. "A Model of Warrant Pricing in a Dynamic Market." *Journal of Finance* 25 (December 1970): 1041.

32. Constantinides, George M. "Strategic Analysis of the Competitive Exercise of Certain Financial Options." *Journal of Economic Theory* 32 (February 1984): 128-138.

33. Galai, Dan and Schneller, Meir I. "Pricing of Warrants and the Value of the Firm." *The Journal of Finance* (December 1978).

34. Giguère, Guynemer. "Warrants—A Mathematical Model of Evaluation." *Analysts Journal* 14, No. 5 (November 1958).

35. Hallingsby, Paul, Jr. "Speculative Opportunities in Stock Purchase Warrants." *Analysts Journal* 3 No. 3 (Third Quarter 1947).

36. Hayes, Samuel L. and Reiling, Henry B. "Sophisticated Financing Tool: The Warrant." *Harvard Business Review* (January-February 1969).

37. Hilliard, Jimmy E. and Leitch, Robert A. "Analysis of the Warrant Hedge in a Stable Paretian Market." *Journal of Financial and Quantitative Analysis* 12 (March 1977): 85-103.

38. Hobbet, Richard D. "Using Stock Warrants in Corporate Acquisitions and Reorganizations." *Journal of Taxation* (March 1958).

39. Kassouf, Sheen T. "Warrant Price Behavior 1945-1964." *Financial Analysts Journal* (January-February 1968).

40. Kassouf, Sheen T. "An Econometric Model for Option Price with Implications for Investors Expectations and Audacity." *Econometrica* (October 1969).

41. Kim, Moon K. and Young, Allan. "Rewards and Risks From Warrant Hedging." *The Journal of Portfolio Management* (Summer 1980).

42. Leabo, D. A. and Rogalski, R. J. "Warrant Price Movements and the Efficient Market Hypotheses." *Journal of Finance* (March 1975).

43. Mayo, Herbert B. "Methods for Comparing Warrants." *Akron Business and Economic Review* (Winter 1973).

44. McKean, Henry P., Jr. "Appendix to Rational Theory of Warrant Pricing: A Free Boundary Problem for the Heat Equation Arising from a Problem in Mathematical Economics." *Industrial Management Review* (Spring 1965): 32-40.

45. Mesler, Donald T. "Investment in Warrants." *AAII Journal* (November 1982): 5-10.

46. Miller, Jerry D. "Accounting for Warrants and Convertible Bonds." *Management Accounting* (January 1973).

47. Miller, Jerry D. "Effects of Longevity on Values of Stock Purchase Warrants." *Financial Analysts Journal:* 27 (November-December 1971) 78.

48. Morrison, Russell J. "The Warrants or the Stock?" *Analysts Journal* 13 No. 5 (November 1957).

49. Noreen, Eric and Wolfson, Mark. "Equilibrium Warrant Pricing Models and Accounting for Executive Stock Options." *Journal of Accounting Research* 19 (Autumn 1981): 384-398.

50. Parkinson, Michael. "Empirical Warrant-Stock Relationships." *The Journal of Business* (October 1972).

51. Pease, Fred. "The Warrant—Its Powers and Its Hazards." *Financial Analysts Journal* 19, No. 1 (January-February 1963).

52. Post, Lawrence A. "Yield to Early Maturity—An Important Factor with Usable Bonds." *Financial Analysts Journal* (November-December 1973).

53. Reiling, Henry B. "Warrants in Bond-Warrant Units: A Survey and Assessment." *Michigan Law Review* (August 1972): 1411-1474.

54. Rogalski, R. J. "Trading in Warrants by Mechanical Systems." *Journal of Finance* (March 1977).

55. Rush, David F. and Melcher, Ronald W. "An Empirical Examination of the Factors Which Influence Warrant Prices." *The Journal of Finance* (December 1973).

56. Samuelson, Paul A. "Rational Theory of Warrant Pricing." *Industrial Management Review* 6 No. 2 (Spring 1965): 29.

57. Samuelson, Paul A. and Merton, Robert C. "A Corporate Model of Warrant Pricing that Maximizes Utility." *Industrial Management Review* (Winter 1969).

58. Schwartz, Eduardo S. "The Valuation of Warrants: Implementing a New Approach." *Journal of Financial Economics* (January 1977).

59. Schwartz, William. "The Advantage Warrants Have—Leverage Prospects." *The Commercial and Financial Chronicle* (March 5, 1970).

60. Schwartz, William. "Warrants: A Form of Equity Capital." *Financial Analysts Journal* (September-October 1970): 87.

61. Shelton, John P. "The Relation of the Price of a Warrant to the Price of Its Associated Stock." *Financial Analysts Journal* Part 1 (May-June 1967): 134-151 and Part 2 (July-August 1967): 88-100.

62. Sinkey, Joseph F. and Miles, James A. "The Use of Warrants in the Bail Out of First Pennsylvania Bank: An Application of Warrant Pricing." *Financial Management* (Autumn 1982): 27-82.

63. Sprenkle, Case. "Warrant Prices as Indicators of Expectations." *Yale Economic Essays* I, No. 2 (1961).

64. Stanton, Thomas C. and Maxwell, Philip H. "Warrants: A Cost of Capital Perspective." *Financial Executive* (September 1980).

65. Stevenson, Richard A. and Lavely, Joe. "Why a Bond Warrant Issue." *Financial Executive* (June 1970): 16-24.

66. Stone, Bernell K. "Warrant Financing." *Journal of Financial and Quantitative Analysis* (March 1976).

67. Strong, Robert A. and Fischetti, Steven V. "Hedging with Stock Warrants: A Free Lunch?" *AAII Journal* (February 1985).

68. Tanner, Dennis A. "Determinants of Excess Return and Skewness in Warrants." *Journal of the Midwest Finance Association* (1974).

69. Turov, Daniel. "Dividend Paying Stocks and Their Warrants." *Financial Analysts Journal* (March-April 1973).

70. Turov, Daniel. "Out of the Cellar—The Market is Down on Real Estate Investment Trust Warrants." *Barron's* (March 27, 1972).

71. Turov, Daniel. "Speculative Security—Warrants, Argues a Fan, Have a Lot Going for Them." *Barron's* (November 28, 1983).

72. Turov, Daniel. "Stock or Warrant? Figuring Out Which One to Buy Can Be Important." *Barron's* (March 9, 1980).

73. Turov, Daniel. "Trampled Rights—Warrant-Holders have Become an Oppressed Minority." *Barron's* (March 19, 1973).

74. Van Horne, J. C. "Warrant Valuation in Relation to Volatility and Opportunity Costs." *Industrial Management Review* (Spring 1969).

75. Whittaker, John. "The Evaluation of Warrants." *Investment Analyst* (UK) (October 1967).

76. Yeasting, Kenneth L. "C D Warrants." *Financial Analysts Journal* (March-April 1970).

INDEX

211

Self-Directed IRAs for the Active Investor: Taking Charge of Building Your Nest Egg, by Peter D. Heerwagen. ISBN 0–917253–32–9.

The Investor's Desktop Portfolio Planner, by Geoffrey Hirt, Stanley Block, and Fred Jury. ISBN 0–917253–33–7.

The New Guide to Tax Sheltered Investments: How To Evaluate and Buy Tax-Favored Investments That Perform, by G. Timothy Haight and John C. Chanoski. ISBN 0–917253–30–2.

The Stock Index Futures Market: A Trader's Insights and Strategies, by B. Thomas Byrne, Jr. ISBN 0–917253–28–0.

The Trader's and Investor's Guide to Commodity Trading Systems, Software and Data Bases, by William T. Taylor. ISBN 0–917253–41–8.

Timing the Market: How to Profit in Bull and Bear Markets with Technical Analysis, by Weiss Research. ISBN 0–917253–37–X.

The Handbook of Mortgage-Backed Securities, by Frank J. Fabozzi. ISBN 0-917253-04-3.

Titles in Business

Revitalizing Your Business: Five Steps to Successfully Turning Around Your Company, by Edmund P. Freiermuth. ISBN 0–917253–05–1.

Compensating Yourself: Personal Income, Benefits and Tax Strategies for Business Owners, by Gerald I. Kalish. ISBN 0–917253–07–8.

Using Consultants: A Consumer's Guide for Managers, by Thomas A. Easton and Ralph Conant. ISBN 0–917253–03–5.

Cutting Loose: Making the Transition From Employee to Entrepreneur, by Thomas A. Easton and Ralph W. Conant. ISBN 0–917253–14–0.

What's What in American Business: Facts and Figures on the Biggest and the Best, by George Kurian. ISBN 0–917253–17–5.

Competing for Clients: The Complete Guide to Marketing and Promoting Professional Services, by Bruce Marcus. ISBN 0–917253–26–4.

Compensating Your Sales Force: The Sales Executive's Book of Compensation Programs and Strategies, by W. G. Ryckman. ISBN 0–917253–38–8.

Leasing Industrial and Business Equipment: Strategies and Techniques for Lessors and Lessees, by Lloyd A. Haynes, Jr. ISBN 0–917253–31–0.

Not Heard on the Street: An Irreverent Dictionary of Wall Street, by Maurice Joy. ISBN 0–917253–40–x.

Public Relations for the Entrepreneur and the Growing Business: How to Use Public Relations to Increase Visibility and Create Opportunities For You and Your Company, by Norman R. Soderberg. ISBN 0-917253-35-3.

The Executive's Guide to Business and Economic Forecasting, by Charles E. Webster. ISBN 0-917253-36-1.

The Entrepreneur's Guide to Capital: More Than 40 Techniques for Capitalizing and Refinancing New and Growing Businesses, by Jennifer Lindsey. ISBN 0-917253-34-5.

The 101 Best Performing Companies in America, by Ronald N. Paul and James W. Taylor. ISBN 0-917253-39-6.

The Operating Executive's Handbook of Profit Planning Tools and Techniques, by Charles J. Woelfel and Charles D. Mecimore. ISBN 0-917253-24-8.

The Valuation of Privately-Held Businesses: State-of-the-Art Techniques for Buyers, Sellers and Their Advisors, by Irving L. Blackman. ISBN 0-917253-27-2.

For more information, contact Probus Publishing Company at (312) 346-7985.